Complete Study Edition | $1.50

King Henry IV, Part 1

Commentary | Complete Text | Glossary

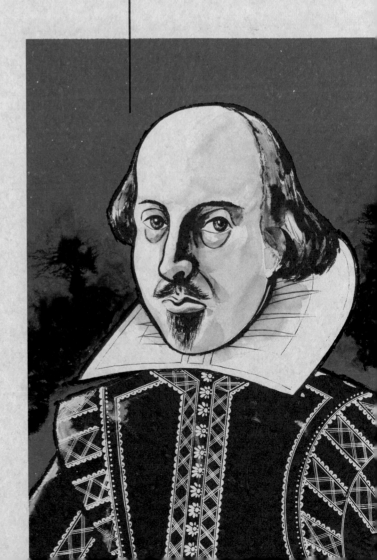

Complete Study Edition

King Henry IV, Part 1

Commentary   Complete Text   Glossary

edited by
SIDNEY LAMB
Associate Professor of English,
Sir George Williams University, Montreal

Cliff's Notes
INCORPORATED

Bethany Station, Lincoln, Nebr. 68505

ISBN 8220-1424-6

Copyright © 1967, 1965

by

C. K. Hillegass

Originally published under the
title "King Henry IV, Part 1:
Complete Study Guide," copyright © 1965.

King Henry IV, Part 1

SHAKESPEARE WAS NEVER MORE MEANINGFUL—

. . . than when read in Cliff's "Complete Study Edition." The introductory sections give you all of the background information about the author and his work necessary for reading with understanding and appreciation. A descriptive bibliography provides guidance in the selection of works for further study. The inviting three-column arrangement of the complete text offers the maximum in convenience to the reader. Adjacent to the text there is a running commentary that provides clear supplementary discussion of the play as it develops. Obscure words and obsolete usages used by Shakespeare are explained in the glosses directly opposite to the line in which they occur. The numerous allusions are also clarified.

SIDNEY LAMB—

. . . the editor of this Shakespeare "Complete Study Edition," attended Andover Academy and Columbia University, receiving the Prince of Wales Medal for Philosophy and the Moyes Travelling Fellowship. Following graduate studies in Elizabethan literature at King's College, Cambridge, from 1949 to 1952, he became a member of the English Faculty of the University of London's University of the Gold Coast in West Africa. Professor Lamb joined the faculty of Sir George Williams University, Montreal, in 1956.

King Henry IV, Part 1

Contents

ath bene sundry times publiquely
ht Honoutable the Lord Cham
his Seruants.

THE MOST EX-
cellent and lamentable
Tragedie, of Romeo
and *Iuliet.*

an introductio

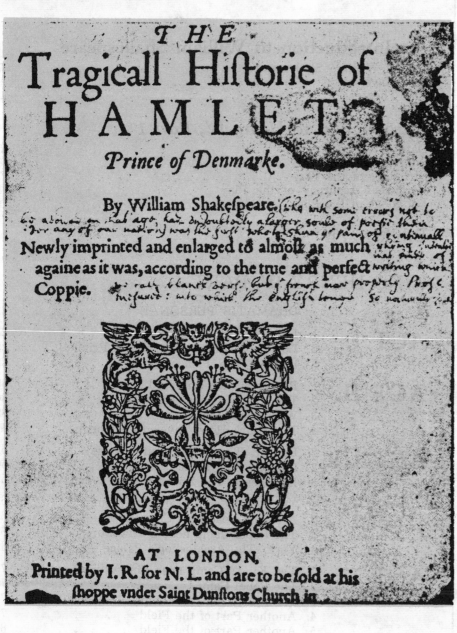

THE
Tragicall Hiſtorie of
HAMLET,
Prince of Denmarke.

By William Shakeſpeare.

Newly imprinted and enlarged to almoſt as much
againe as it was, according to the true and perfect
Coppie.

AT LONDON,
Printed by I. R. for N. L. and are to be ſold at his
ſhoppe vnder Saint Dunſtons Church in

Two books are essential to the library of any English-speaking household; one of these is the Bible and the other is the works of William Shakespeare. These books form part of the house furnishings, not as reading material generally, but as the symbols of religion and culture—sort of a twentieth-century counterpart of the ancient Roman household gods. This symbolic status has done a great deal of damage both to religion and to Shakespeare.

Whatever Shakespeare may have been, he was not a deity. He was a writer of popular plays, who made a good living, bought a farm in the country, and retired at the age of about forty-five to enjoy his profits as a gentleman. The difference between Shakespeare and the other popular playwrights of his time was that he wrote better plays —plays that had such strong artistic value that they have been popular ever since. Indeed, even today, if Shakespeare could col-

6

William
to Shakespeare

lect his royalties, he would be among the most prosperous of playwrights.

During the eighteenth century but mostly in the nineteenth, Shakespeare's works became "immortal classics," and the cult of Shakespeare-worship was inaugurated. The plays were largely removed from their proper place on the stage into the library where they became works of literature rather than drama and were regarded as long poems, attracting all the artistic and psuedo-artistic atmosphere surrounding poetry. In the nineteenth century this attitude was friendly but later, and especially in the early twentieth century, a strange feeling arose in the English-speaking world that poetry was sissy stuff, not for men but for "pansies" and women's clubs. This of course is sheer nonsense.

This outline will present a detailed analysis of the play and background information which will show the play in its proper perspective. This means seeing the play in relation to the other plays, to the history of the times when they were written, and in relation to the theatrical technique required for their successful performance.

G. B. Harrison's book *Introducing Shakespeare*, published by Penguin Books, will be of value for general information about Shakespeare and his plays. For reference material on the Elizabethan Theater, consult E. K. Chambers, *The Elizabethan*

Theatre (four volumes). For study of the organization and production methods of this theater see *Henslowe's Diary* edited by W. W. Greg. Again for general reading the student will enjoy Margaret Webster's *Shakespeare Without Tears,* published by Whittlesey House (Mc-Graw-Hill) in 1942.

The remainder of the Introduction will be divided into sections discussing Shakespeare's life, his plays, and his theater.

LIFE OF WILLIAM SHAKESPEARE

From the standpoint of one whose main interest lies with the plays themselves, knowledge of Shakespeare's life is not very important. Inasmuch as it treats of the period between 1592 and 1611, when the plays were being written, knowledge of his life is useful in that it may give some clues as to the topical matters introduced into the plays. For instance, the scene of Hamlet's advice to the players (Act III Scene ii) takes on an added significance when considered along with the fame and bombastic style of Edward Alleyn, the then famous actor-manager of the Lord Admiral's Players (the most powerful rivals of Shakespeare's company).

This biography is pieced together from the surviving public records of the day, from contemporary references in print, and from the London Stationer's Register. It is by no means complete. The skeletal nature of the

biographical material available to scholars has led commentators in the past to invent part of the story to fill it out. These parts have frequently been invented by men who were more interested in upholding a private theory than in telling the truth, and this habit of romancing has led to a tradition of inaccurate Shakespearian biography. For this reason this outline may be of use in disposing of bad traditions.

In the heyday of the self-made man, the story developed that Shakespeare was a poor boy from the village, virtually uneducated, who fled from Stratford to London to escape prosecution for poaching on the lands of Sir Thomas Lucy, and there by his talent and a commendable industry raised himself to greatness. This rags-to-riches romance was in the best Horatio Alger tradition but was emphatically not true. The town records of Stratford make it clear that John Shakespeare, father of the playwright, was far from a pauper. He was a wealthy and responsible citizen who held in turn several municipal offices. He married (1557) Mary Arden, the daughter of a distinguished Catholic family. William, their third son, was baptized in the Parish Church in 1564. He had a good grammar school education. Ben Jonson's remark that Shakespeare had "small Latin and less Greek" did not mean the same in those days, when the educated man had a fluent command of

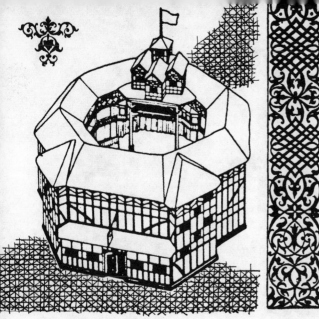

Exterior view of "The Globe"

Shakespeare's London

Interior view of "The Globe"

an introduction to Shakespeare

Latin and probably at least a reading knowledge of Greek, as it does now when classical scholars are few. The remark has been construed by the Horatio Alger people as meaning that Shakespeare reached London a semi-literate bumpkin; it is nonsense. It means merely that Shakespeare was not a university man, as most of the writers were, and that the University Wits were taking out their jealousy in snobbery and pointing out that Shakespeare used less purely literary symbolism than they did.

Shakespeare married Ann Hathaway when he was eighteen years old. She was some years older than he and the marriage seems to have been a rather hasty affair. Five months after the marriage, Suzanna, the first child, was born. Two years later, in 1585, twins Hamnet and Judith were baptized.

No one knows when Shakespeare came to London. The first mention of him occurs in the bad-tempered pamphlet which Robert Greene, one of the University Wits and a famous playwright, wrote just before his death. Greene complains of "an upstart crow, beautified with our feathers, that with his tiger's heart wrapped in a player's hide, supposes he is as well able to bombast out a blank verse as the best of you; and being an absolute Yohannes factotum, is in his own conceit the only Shakescene in a country." This was written in 1592 and indicates not only that Shakespeare was in

London at the time, but that he was writing plays and beginning to make such a name for himself as to call forth the jealous apprehension of an established writer.

The next year, 1593, was a year of plague, and by order of the Lord Mayor and the Aldermen, the theaters were closed. The players, disorganized by this action, went on tour outside of London. During this year Shakespeare's two long poems, *Venus and Adonis* and *The Rape of Lucrece,* were entered in the Stationer's Register. Both were dedicated to the Earl of Southampton.

The public theaters had not been established very long. The first of these, called the Theatre, was built for James Burbage in 1576. By 1594, there were three such theaters in London, the two new houses being the Curtain and the Rose. By 1594, also, the three most celebrated of the writers, Kyd, Greene, and Marlowe were dead, and Shakespeare had already a considerable reputation. Before this date the theaters had been largely low class entertainment and the plays had been of rather poor quality. Through the revival of classical drama in the schools (comedies) and the Inns of Court (tragedies), an interest had been created in the stage. The noblemen of the time were beginning to attend the public theaters, and their tastes demanded a better class of play.

Against the background of this

FLUVIUS

South warke

3   4   5

increasing status and upper-class popularity of the theaters, Shakespeare's company was formed. After the 1594 productions under Alleyn, this group of actors divided. Alleyn formed a company called the Lord Admiral's Company which played in Henslowe's Rose Theatre. Under the leadership of the Burbages (James was the owner of the Theatre and his son Richard was a young tragic actor of great promise), Will Kemp (the famous comedian), and William Shakespeare, the Lord Chamberlain's company came into being. This company continued throughout Shakespeare's career. It was renamed in 1603, shortly after Queen Elizabeth's death, becoming the King's players.

The company played at the Theatre until Burbage's lease on the land ran out. The landlord was not willing to come to satisfactory terms. The company moved across the river and built the new Globe theater. The principal sharers in the new place were Richard and Cuthbert Burbage each with two and a half shares and William Shakespeare, John Heminge, Angustus Phillips, Thomas Pope, and Will Kemp, each with one share.

Burbage had wanted to establish a private theater and had rented the refectory of the old Blackfriars' monastery. Not being allowed to use this building he leased it to a man called Evans who obtained permission to produce plays acted by chil-dren. This venture was so successful as to make keen competition for the existing companies. This vogue of child actors is referred to in *Hamlet,* Act II Scene ii.

The children continued to play at Blackfriars until, in 1608, their license was suspended because of the seditious nature of one of their productions. By this time the public attitude towards the theaters had changed, and Burbage's Company, now the King's players, could move into the Blackfriars theater.

Partners with the Burbages in this enterprise were Shakespeare, Heminge, Condell, Sly, and Evans. This was an indoor theater, whereas the Globe had been outdoors. The stage conditions were thus radically altered. More scenery could be used; lighting effects were possible. Shakespeare's works written for this theater show the influence of change in conditions.

To return to the family affairs of the Shakespeares, records show that in 1596 John Shakespeare was granted a coat of arms and, along with his son, was entitled to call himself "gentleman." In this year also, William Shakespeare's son Hamnet died. In 1597 William Shakespeare bought from William Underwood a sizable estate at Stratford, called New Place.

Shakespeare's father died in 1601, his mother, in 1608. Both of his daughters married, one in 1607, the other in 1616.

During this time, Shakespeare went on acquiring property in Stratford. He retired to New Place probably around 1610 although this date is not definitely established, and his career as a dramatist was practically at an end. *The Tempest,* his last complete play, was written around the year 1611.

The famous will, in which he left his second best bed to his wife, was executed in 1616 and later on in that same year he was buried.

THE PLAYS

Thirty-seven plays are customarily included in the works of William Shakespeare. Scholars have been at great pains to establish the order in which these plays were written. The most important sources of information for this study are the various records of performances which exist, the printed editions which came out during Shakespeare's career, and such unmistakable references to current events as may crop up in the plays. The effect of the information gathered in this way is generally to establish two dates between which a given play must have been written. In *Hamlet* for instance, there is a scene in which Hamlet refers to the severe competition given to the adult actors by the vogue for children's performances. This vogue first became a serious threat to the professional companies in about 1600. In 1603 a very bad edition was published, without authorization, of *The*

Elizabethan types

Lute, standing cup, stoop

Queen Elizabeth

an introduction to Shakespeare

Tragical History of Hamlet, Prince of Denmark by William Shakespeare. These two facts indicate that *Hamlet* was written between the years of 1600 and 1603. This process fixed the order in which most of the plays were written. Those others of which no satisfactory record could be found were inserted in their logical place in the series according to the noticeable development of Shakespeare's style. In these various ways we have arrived at the following chronological listing of the plays.

1591 *Henry VI Part I*
Henry VI Part II
Henry VI Part III
Richard III
Titus Andronicus
Love's Labour Lost
The Two Gentlemen of Verona
The Comedy of Errors
The Taming of the Shrew

1594 *Romeo and Juliet*
A Midsummer Night's Dream
Richard II
King John
The Merchant of Venice

1597 *Henry IV Part I*
Henry IV Part II
Much Ado About Nothing
Merry Wives of Windsor
As You Like It
Julius Caesar
Henry V
Troilus and Cressida

1601 *Hamlet*
Twelfth Night
Measure for Measure
All's Well That Ends Well

Othello

1606 *King Lear*
Macbeth
Timon of Athens
Antony and Cleopatra
Coriolanus

1609 *Pericles*

1611 *Cymbeline*
The Winter's Tale
The Tempest
Henry VIII

At this point it is pertinent to review the tradition of dramatic form that had been established before Shakespeare began writing. Drama in England sprang at the outset from the miracle and morality plays of the medieval guilds. These dramatized Bible stories became increasingly less religious as time passed until finally they fell into disrepute. The next development was the writing of so-called *interludes*. These varied in character but often took the form of bawdy farce. As the renaissance gathered force in England, Roman drama began to be revived at the schools and the Inns of Court. Before long English writers were borrowing plots and conventions wholesale from the classic drama. The Italian model was the most fashionable and consequently was largely adopted, but many features of the old *interludes* still persisted, especially in plays written for the public theaters.

With the development among the nobility of a taste for the theater, a higher quality of work became in demand. Very few of

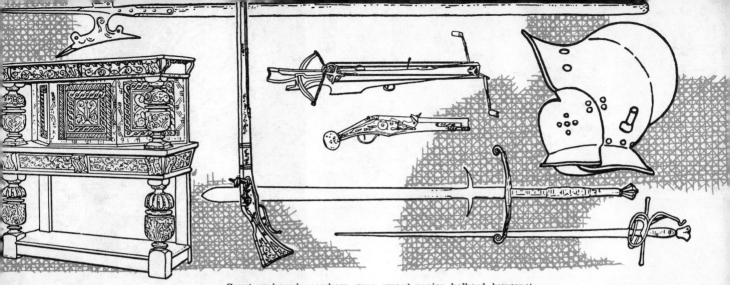

Court cupboard, crossbow, guns, sword, rapier, halberd, burgonet

the very early plays have survived. The reason for this is that the plays were not printed to be read; no one considered them worth the trouble. A play was strung together out of a set of stock characters and situations with frantic haste, often by as many as a dozen different men. These men who worked on plays did not regard their writing activity as of prime importance. They were primarily actors. With the cultivation of taste for better plays came the idea that the work of a playwright was an effort demanding special skill. The highborn audiences were interested in the plays themselves and began to include editions of their favorite plays in their libraries. With this demand for printed copies of the plays, the conception began of the dramatist as an artist in his own right, whether or not he acted himself (as most of them did).

By 1592, when Shakespeare began to make his personal reputation, a set of traditions had developed. This body of traditions gave Shakespeare the basic materials with which to work.

A special type of comedy writing had developed, centered around the name of John Lyly, designed for the sophisticated audience of the court and presented with lavish dances and decorative effects. This type of play was characterized by a delicately patterned artificiality of speech. The dialogue was studded with complicated references to Latin and Italian literature that the renaissance had made fashionable.

Shakespeare used this method extensively. In the early plays (before *The Merchant of Venice*) he was experimenting and wrote much that is nothing more than conventional. Later on, as his mature style developed, the writing becomes integral with and indispensable to the play and no longer appears artificial. In *Romeo and Juliet,* an early play, the following lines are spoken by Lady Capulet in urging Juliet to accept the Count Paris for her husband. These lines are brilliant but artificial, and the play seems to pause in order that this trick bit of word-acrobatics may be spoken.

Read o'er the volume of young
    Paris' face,
And find delight, writ there
    with beauty's pen.
Examine every married lineament,
And see how one another lends
    content:
And what obscured in this fair
    volume lies,
Find written in the margent of
    his eyes.
This precious book of love, this
    unbound lover,
To beautify him only needs a
    cover!

The other most important dramatic tradition was that of tragedy. The Elizabethan audiences liked spectacular scenes; they also had a great relish for scenes of sheer horror. This led to a school of tragic writing made popular by Kyd and Marlowe.

These plays were full of action and color and incredible wickedness, and the stage literally ran with artificial blood. Shakespeare's early tragedies are directly in this tradition, but later the convention becomes altered and improved in practice, just as that of comedy had done. The scene in *King Lear* where Gloucester has his eyes torn out stems from this convention. Lear, however, is a comparatively late play and the introduction of this scene does not distort or interrupt its organization.

Shakespeare's stylistic development falls into a quite well-defined progression. At first he wrote plays according to the habit of his rivals. He very quickly began experimenting with his technique. His main concern seems to be with tricks of language. He was finding out just what he could do. These early plays use a great deal of rhyme, seemingly just because Shakespeare liked writing rhyme. Later on, rhyme is used only when there is a quite definite dramatic purpose to justify it. Between the early plays and those which may be called mature (*The Merchant of Venice* is the first of the mature plays), there is a basic change in method. In the early works Shakespeare was taking his patterns from previous plays and writing his own pieces, quite consciously incorporating one device here and another there.

In the later period these tricks of the trade had been tested and

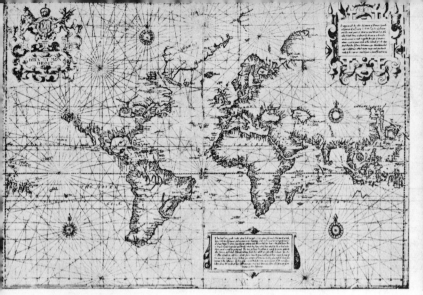

The world as known in 1600

Elizabethan coins

absorbed; they had become not contrived methods but part of Shakespeare's mind. This meant that, quite unconsciously, while his total attention was focused on the emotional and intellectual business of writing a masterpiece, he wrote in terms of the traditional habits he had learned and used in the earlier period. (*Henry IV*, *Julius Caesar*, *Henry V*, and *Hamlet* are the plays of this advanced stage.)

The group of plays between 1606 and 1609 shows a further new development. Having reached mastery of his medium in terms of dramatic technique (with *Othello*) and of power over the tension of thought in moving easily through scenes of comedy, pathos, and tragedy, he turned again to the actual literary quality of his plays and began to enlarge his scope quite beyond and apart from the theatrical traditions of his day. The early results of this new attempt are the two plays *King Lear* and *Macbeth*. The change in these plays is in the direction of concentration of thought. The attempt is, by using masses of images piled one on another, to convey shadings and intensities of emotion not before possible. He was trying to express the inexpressible. For example the following is from the last part of

an introduction
to Shakespeare

Lady Macbeth's famous speech in Act I, Scene v:

> Come, thick night,
> And pall thee in the dunnest smoke of hell,
> That my keen knife see not the wound it makes,
> Nor heaven peep through the blanket of the dark,
> To cry, hold, hold!

Compare the concentrated imagery of this speech with Hamlet's soliloquy at the end of Act III, Scene ii.

> 'Tis now the very witching time of night,
> When churchyards yawn, and hell itself breathes out
> Contagion to this world: now could I drink hot blood,
> And do such bitterness as the day
> Would quake to look on.

The sentiment of these two speeches is similar, but the difference in method is striking and produces a difference again in the type of effect. The *Lear-Macbeth* type of writing produces a higher tension of subtlety but tends to collect in masses rather than to move in lines as the lighter, more transparent writing of *Hamlet* does.

Shakespeare's last plays were conceived for the new indoor theater at Blackfriars and show this is in a more sophisticated type of staging. In *The Tempest*, last and most celebrated of these late comedies, there is dancing, and much complicated staging (such as the disappearing banquet, the ship at sea, and so on). The writing of plays for the

more distinguished audience of Blackfriars, and the increased stage resources there provided, influenced the form of the plays.

The writing of these plays forms a culmination. In his early apprenticeship Shakespeare had been extravagant in word-acrobatics, testing the limits of his technique. In the Lear-Macbeth period of innovation he had tried the limits of concentrated emotion to the point almost of weakening the dramatic effectiveness of the plays. In *The Tempest* his lines are shaken out into motion again. He seems to have been able to achieve the subtlety he was after in verse of light texture and easy movement, no longer showing the tendency to heaviness or opacity visible in *King Lear* and *Macbeth*.

THE THEATER

The first public theater in London was built in the year 1576 for James Burbage and was called simply The Theatre. Before this time players' companies had performed for the public in the courtyards of the city inns. For a more select public they frequently played in the great halls of institutions, notably the Inns of Court. The stage and auditorium of the Elizabethan theater were based on these traditions and combined features of both the hall and the inn-yard. The auditorium was small. There was a pit where the orchestra seats would be in a modern playhouse; this section was for the lowest classes who stood during the performances. Around the

12

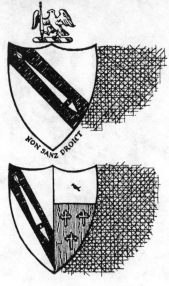

Shakespeare's Coat of Arms

Wood cut camp illustration

wall was a gallery for the gentry. The galleries and the tiring-house behind the fore-stage were roofed; the rest was open to the sky. The stage consisted of a very large platform that jutted out so that the pit audience stood on three sides of it. Behind this, under the continuation behind the stage of the gallery, was the inner stage; this was supplied with a curtain, but the open fore-stage was not. Above this inner stage was a balcony (really a continuation of the gallery), forming still another curtained stage. This gallery was used for kings addressing subjects from balconies, for the storming of walls, for Juliet's balcony and bedroom, for Cleopatra's monument and so on. Costumes and properties were extravagant (such as guillotines, fountains, ladders, etc.); extensive music was constantly used and such sound effects as cannon, drums, or unearthly screams were common; but there was no painted scenery as we know it; there was no darkness to focus attention on the stage, no facilities for stage-lighting. All these things are in marked contrast to the modern stage conventions and thus a serious problem of adaptation is posed when it comes to producing the plays under present day conditions.

The advantages are not all with the modern stage. It is true that the modern or picture stage can do more in the way of realistic effects, but this kind of realism is not important to good drama. In fact there has been a recent trend away from realistic scenery in the theater back to a conventional or stylized simplicity.

One effect of Shakespeare's stage upon his work was to make the scenes in the plays more person-scenes than place-scenes. As a matter of fact in many cases the places assigned in the texts to various scenes were not in the original and have only been added by an editor who did not understand this very fact.

It used to be said that *Antony and Cleopatra* could not be staged and was written to be read rather than acted. The grounds for this statement were that in the fourth act there were no less than fourteen scenes. To some, a scene means a change of place and requires a break in the play while scenery is shifted. To Shakespeare these scenes meant no such thing; they meant, simply, that there were fourteen different groupings of people, successively and without any break, carrying on the action of the play. The scene headings when added should have been (1) Caesar, (2) Antony and Cleopatra, (3) the common soldiers, etc., instead of (1) Before Alexandria, (2) Alexandria, a room in the palace, etc. By this you may see that with all its limitations, the Elizabethan stage had a measure of flexibility that the modern stage could envy.

Fashions in staging Shakespeare have altered radically in the last few years. At the close of the nineteenth century, Sir Herbert Beerbohm Tree staged a spectacular series of pageant productions. All the tricks of romantic realistic staging were used and, if necessary, the play was twisted, battered, and re-written to accommodate the paraphernalia.

The modern method is to produce the plays as nearly according to the text as possible and work out a compromise to achieve the sense of space and of flexibility necessary, yet without departing so far from the stage habits of today as to confuse or divert the audience. This technique was inaugurated by Granville-Barker in the early twentieth century. With the exception of such extravagant stunts as Orson Welles' production of *Julius Caesar* in modern dress (set in Chicago and complete with tommy-guns), the prevailing practice now is to use simple, stylized scenery adapted to the needs of producing the play at full length.

Much can be done in the way of learning Shakespeare through books, but the only sure way is to see a well produced performance by a good company of actors. Whatever genius Shakespeare may have possessed as a psychologist, philosopher, or poet, he was first of all a man of the theater, who knew it from the inside, and who wrote plays so well-plotted for performance that from his day up to the present, no great actor has been able to resist them.

an introduction

INTRODUCTION TO HENRY IV, PART 1

One of Shakespeare's aims in writing this play was to follow up the success he previously had with *Richard II,* which may well be regarded as the precursor of *Henry IV, Part I.* This play is followed by *Henry IV, Part II,* and by *Henry V,* thus completing the cycle. Several incidents referred to in *Richard II* crop up again in *Henry IV, Part I,* and the central figure, Henry Bolingbroke, is common to both; the Prince Hal of *Henry IV, Part I* is the monarch in *Henry V.* Shakespeare probably did not originally intend to write a series of historical plays neatly fitting together in this manner, since *Richard II* is very different in tone and treatment from the other plays in what did, in effect, become a series.

In the play *Richard II,* Henry Bolingbroke, son and heir of John of Gaunt (fourth son of Edward III), accuses Thomas Mowbray (Duke of Norfolk) of treason. They are about to settle the matter by personal combat when King Richard intervenes and banishes them both from his kingdom. Mowbray is banished for life, Bolingbroke for only six years: this action shows whom the King favored. King Richard confiscates all John of Gaunt's lands and revenues when the noble old man dies (after rebuking Richard for

his poor housekeeping, which is likely to bankrupt the kingdom, "this royal throne of kings"), then sets sail for Ireland to crush a rebellion there. In his absence, Richard's uncle (the Duke of York) is appointed protector of the kingdom, and the Earl of Northumberland and his impetuous son, Hotspur, stay behind because they suspect that Bolingbroke will soon be returning to claim his father's (i.e., John of Gaunt's) lands and revenues.

Henry Bolingbroke lands at Ravenspurgh (a port which actually existed, but which has since been silted up) and is met by Northumberland, and later by York and Hotspur. He swears that he has come back only to claim the property that has been wrongly taken from him, together with the Dukedom of Lancaster to which he is now entitled, but it soon becomes clear that he is after the Crown of England. The common people acclaimed him, and he made his way amid an enthusiastic throng who invited him to take power. Richard hastens back from Ireland to find himself deserted and betrayed. He surrenders to Bolingbroke, and is retired to Pomfret Castle, where he was murdered shortly after by Sir Pierce Exton, at the request of the new King. Richard's murder at Pomfret marks the climax of the play *Richard II,* and Henry Bolingbroke becomes the reign-

he History of King Henry IV, Part 1

ing monarch (Henry IV) of *Henry IV, Part I*. This King's son is the reigning monarch (Henry V) of *Henry IV, Part II* and, of course, of *Henry V*. In *Henry IV, Part I* he is called Prince Hal (or Prince of Wales).

In studying *Henry IV, Part I*, it is helpful to keep in mind the following groups:

GROUP 1: THE ROYAL COURT (Henry IV and his followers).

GROUP 2: THE REBELS (Northumberland and Hotspur).

GROUP 3: THE COMIC CHARACTERS (Falstaff and the low life characters).

These three groups are quite loosely interconnected in various ways, and the story of their interconnections constitutes the plot of the play. This play is much less compactly structured than the tragedies of Shakespeare, but provides us with some loveable characters, most notorious of whom is the immortal Falstaff. Nevertheless, though Falstaff is perhaps the most memorable and humorous character in this play, he is not the hero: this position is undubitably occupied by the Prince. It is the Prince's function to help *link* all three centers of interest in this play.

DATE OF COMPOSITION

In the First Folio of 1623, compiled by Shakespeare's friends after the playwright's death, the section containing the so-called *HISTORIES* contained one play the full title of which takes up several lines, namely: *THE HISTORY OF HENRIE THE FOURTH; WITH THE BATTELL OF SHREWSBURIE, BETWEENE THE KING AND LORD HENRY PERCIE SURNAMED HENRIE HOTSPUR OF THE NORTH. WITH THE HUMOROUS CONCEITS OF SIR JOHN FALSTALFFE.* This is the play that was probably first produced during the theatrical season of 1597-98.

The term "histories" was intended to distinguish those plays which deal with English history from other plays, usually tragedies, which take their plots from events in Greek or Roman history. But since there is much in *Henry IV, Part I* which is probably not true to history (the matter of historical accuracy is discussed later) it would, perhaps, be better to call this play a *Chronicle*, or even a *Pageant*. It is sometimes staged as a *Tableau Vivant*—that is, a living spectacle—but there is too much character play and character development to justify calling the play this.

The Elizabethans were used to chronicle plays, and liked them. Chronicle plays were, however, virtually unknown in Europe at this time. They usually consisted of mere successions of scenes dealing with

some reign or episode in English history, with little or no attempt made to mold the material obtained from the history books, or chronicles, into dramatic form. The chronicle plays were the chief means of communicating historical information to massive audiences, though they frequently and inevitably communicated political bias and gross distortions of truth as well. The documentary war film is the direct descendant of the chronicle plays of old, and it possesses their strengths and weaknesses.

It is not difficult to connect the chronicle play, with its teaching and moralizing function, with the older morality plays, the most famous of which is *Everyman*. The Tudor period was interested in power politics centering upon the throne and its succession, and the historians whose ideas Shakespeare reflected in his plays believed that history should be represented to demonstrate moral instruction and guidance. This view of history has passed away in most western universities, but continues to be preached from the pulpit in many cases.

It was not edifying for the Prince of Wales to spend so much time with rascals and knaves like Sir John Falstaff, but to show him playing a trick on Falstaff and then to show his conversion from knavery to du-

tifulness and responsibility is a profoundly moving moral spectacle. In this way, *Henry IV, Part I* belongs to the moral tradition of the ancient moralities. Yet its characterization is not as stiff, nor its scenes as disconnected, as the earlier three parts of *Henry VI*. It is more coherent than they, but not as coherent (in the structural and developmental senses) as the tragedies.

Henry IV represents neither a work of Shakespeare's youth, nor a work of his maturity, but a good piece of craftsmanship undertaken to prepare him for the more complex works to come.

SOURCES OF THE PLOT

Sir Max Beerbohm's gently wicked wit depicts Shakespeare, creeping up behind a person dressed in earlier garb, and stealing a manuscript from the open pocket; this caricature is called "Shakespeare's method of work." The person from whom Shakespeare is stealing the manuscript is probably Holinshed, although he might be one of half a dozen (or more) others. Was Shakespeare dishonest, did he plagiarize? The question is an intriguing one. He certainly drew upon several sources when writing *Henry IV, Part I*. These sources are usually considered to be Holinshed's *Chronicles* (first published in 1577 although Shakespeare probably used the later edition of 1586-87); Hall's *Chronicle* (published in 1542); Stow's *Annals* (published in 1580); *The Famous Victories of Henry V* (authorship unknown, date probably earlier than 1588); and Daniel's *Civil Wars* (pub-

lished in 1595).

Shakespeare changed and modified his sources, as we shall see when we discuss the historical accuracy of the play.

Sir Walter Raleigh's book *History of the World* struck the same note that Shakespeare strikes at the opening of *Henry IV, Part I*. Part of Raleigh's Preface follows:

The King [Henry IV] whose title was weak and his obtaining of the crown was traitorous; who broke faith with the Lords at his landing, protesting only to intend the recovery of his proper inheritance . . . after that he had enjoyed the realm some few years, was never free from conspiracies and rebellions; he saw (If souls immortal see . . .) his grand child Henry VI and his son the Prince suddenly and without mercy murdered; the possession of the crown (for which he had caused so much blood to be poured out) transferred from his race; and by the issues of his enemies worn and enjoyed . . .

Note the emotionally charged language and the very evident bias; how different from the watered-down "objectivity" cultivated by today's "scientific" historians. Shakespeare took over Raleigh's facts and prejudices, but did not leave them at that; he raised these purely political and historical issues by the exercise of his creative imagination and the beauty and power of his dramatic poetry, to the level of a work of art. Is this dishonesty? Is this plagiarism? The student may answer for himself.

THE TEXT

Since Shakespeare wrote his plays for the immediate use of actors, he was concerned to see that they received a masterscript so that they could make copies of their own parts, with their cues. This copying was done hurriedly with little respect for punctuation, or even verbal or metrical accuracy. When the actor had learned his lines by heart, he frequently threw away the script. Later, if a script were needed for another actor, the words might be written out from memory by the actor who remembered them best. In this way, no accurate edition of the plays was available. In 1623 the First Folio was published by Shakespeare's friends and acquaintances who had to rely on actors' scripts and their own and others' memories. Some expert editing had to be done, and the problems of variant readings and scholarly preferences came into existence. Many Elizabethan plays (some famous ones, too) were never printed at all, or have been lost. It is conceivable that some of Shakespeare's plays have been lost, and the possibility of making an important literary "find" remains to tantalize the bibliophiles and other literary antiquarians.

Henry IV, Part I was first printed in 1598 in quarto form. This is called Q by scholars (from the word quarto, which means having four leaves or eight pages to the sheet). Five other editions, called Q2 to Q6, were published before the *First Folio edition* (known as F) was issued in 1623. A fragment of an

earlier edition than Q was discovered at Bristol, and named Q°, it originally appearing in 1548. Our present text is based on the *First Folio edition*, but the spelling has been modernized for ease of reading. For the original spelling, it is fascinating to consult the text of this play in the photographic facsimile of the *First Folio edition* prepared by Helge Kökeritz and Charles Tyler Prouty: *Published according to the True Originall Copies* by Yale University Press and available from most good public reference libraries.

THE STRUCTURE OF THE PLAY

Henry IV, Part I is a five-act structure consisting of three central issues, or themes, which are expressed dramatically by three central groups of people and their necessary interactions. The first group consists of King Henry IV (the Henry Bolingbroke, who became Duke of Lancaster in the play *Richard II*) and his faithful court, including his two sons, Henry, Prince of Wales and John of Lancaster, the Earl of Westmoreland, Sir Walter Blunt, and their retainers. There is tension within this group for two reasons: Henry IV is aware of conspiracy in the north of England and rebellion on the Welsh border; and his son and heir, who should have been setting an example by taking responsibility, has been cavorting with n'er-do-wells, like Sir John Falstaff, to the exclusion of his serious duties as a royal prince. The second group is that of the conspirators who become rebels. Led by the senior Henry Percy, Earl of Northumberland, but in-

spired by Machiavellian Thomas Percy, Earl of Worcester, this group (which includes the forthright, impetuous, but ingenuous young Henry Percy, surnamed Hotspur) is conspiring with the discontented Scottish nobles in the north, and with the equally discontented and nationalistic Welsh, led by a fiery Celt called Owen Glendower, to usurp the English throne and place thereon the man who, to them, should rightfully be King, Richard II's choice, Edmund Mortimer, Earl of March. Mortimer had been taken prisoner on the Welsh border by Owen Glendower, and had taken the opportunity of marrying Glendower's daughter. The Earl of Douglas (Archibald) and Richard Scroop, Archbishop of York, also belong to the conspiratorial group, but for different reasons.

The third group is put in chiefly for comic relief from the seriousness of the other two groups, and consists of Sir John Falstaff, the Prince of Wales in certain light moods, Mistress Quickly, and such characters of low life as Poins, Gadshill, Peto, and Bardolph.

Shakespeare employs several devices to bring these groups together, to divide them, and, above all, to give them that rather loose coherence which characterizes this history play. Thus, Prince Hal plays a part in all three groups, as fellow-cavorter with Falstaff and his group at the beginning, and as parodist of his father, Henry IV in the famous scene in which he permits Falstaff to rebuke him as Henry IV was later to do, before their reconciliation. This is

comic, but it also relates the serious court group to the low life characters. When Hal plays the trick on Falstaff and later permits Falstaff to tell those magnificent lies to extricate (implicate?) himself, the connection and the separation of these two groups is further reinforced. *Qui s'excuse, s'accuse.* Hal is a young warrior of exactly the same age as the rebel Hotspur, and this fact (coupled with their joint interest in honor) serves to unite them, though they are on opposite sides. The interest they take in each other makes each one more interesting to us, so that when they meet in mortal combat on the battlefield the audience is prepared for a climax ending with the death of one of them. This parallelism is a further coherency device. Falstaff also distinguishes himself on the field of battle, though in less heroic fashion. The very idea of his going to war as commander of an infantry group is ludicrous in itself, and comic in its consequences. Worcester reveals how he had tricked the honorable Hotspur into aiding and abetting the rebels' cause; then the audience realizes what, perhaps, it always felt (because Shakespeare intended it): that Hotspur was the soul of honor, but had the misfortune to be on the wrong side through no fault of his own; thus Hotspur is vindicated.

Many questions involving honor, duty, loyalty and responsibility are raised in subtle ways by Shakespeare in *Henry IV, Part I*, but perhaps the answers are in the speech by Falstaff

on the nature of honor; in the character of Falstaff contrasted with the character of the Prince; and in their actions, and the consequences of those actions. We remember Falstaff, but not as hero; there is only one hero in this play, and Shakespeare leaves us in no doubt as to who he is: the Prince.

THE HISTORICAL ACCURACY OF THE PLAY

Suppose that this play is found, after examination, to be historically inaccurate and to embody and thereby perpetuate distortions and prejudices. This certainly does not mean that it is necessarily bad entertainment. We do not usually require stage plays and other forms of entertainment to be historically accurate. We do not object to comedians being wildly inaccurate when they present a skit on politics. Why, then, should we require historical accuracy in *Henry IV, Part I*, when after all, this play is called a History: this simply means that it deals in a creative and imaginative manner with episodes taken from English history. There is no obligation on the writer to engage in detailed historical research to make sure that he has his facts right. Tudor historians favored the sweeping generalization, the anti-Richard, pro-Bolingbroke theme. They were pro-Henry IV (with few exceptions) and anti-Percy, and so, by and large, were most Elizabethans. So was Shakespeare, fortunately, for this attitude enabled him to give them a play reinforcing all their own prejudices, thereby insuring popularity and conse-

quently a profitable boxoffice return.

Where, though, did Shakespeare take liberties with his source material and, therefore, with historical fact and interpretation? In the first place, he juggled ages. In the play Prince Hal and Hotspur are the same age: this similiarity is pleasing to an audience ingenuous enough to prefer pleasing but unlikely parallelisms of chronology. In fact (historically) Prince Hal was only fourteen years old while Hotspur was middle-aged. But if Shakespeare had left it like that, we would have been spared those flattering comparisons, all the suspense, and finally the exciting combat on the battlefield. The dramatic balance of this play actually depends on the parallelism of ages between the Prince and Hal. King Henry IV had to be years older than the two boys, yet historically we are told that Hotspur was two years older than the King. History is evidently no artist, she does not know how to tidy-up the loose ends, but Shakespeare did.

Shakespeare had no scruples about advancing the age of King Henry IV, thus he makes the King speak like an old man, "crushing *our old limbs* in ungentle steel" when, at the time of the Battle of Shrewsbury, Bolingbroke was only in his thirties.

Shakespeare delays historical episodes to suit his own dramatic purposes; thus the meeting and reconciliation between King Henry IV and Prince Hal takes place earlier in Holinshed's

Chronicles than it does in *Henry IV, Part I*. This delay is needed to give the Prince time to play the trick on Falstaff, and to play out the King's wrath with Falstaff after the lying episode, *before* the royal reconciliation would have been artistically right. Since the reconciliation is the turning point of the play, it was necessary to precede it with some action to preserve the dramatic balance of the whole.

There is some uncertainty in the old writers about whether the King was rescued from mortal combat during the Battle of Shrewsbury, or whether he extricated himself, or, if he was rescued, exactly who did the rescuing. Yet Shakespeare blithely makes the Prince rescue his father, which puts Oedipus to shame and disconcerts those historians who disagree with the historian Daniel.

Shakespeare did not trouble to research details concerning where meetings took place. The meeting between Henry IV and Hotspur took place in London, in the play; but actually it was held at Windsor Castle.

Shakespeare confused two characters who bore the same name, but so did Holinshed. Historically there were two Edmund Mortimers: the young Edmund Mortimer, Hotspur's brother-in-law, is confused with that Edmund Mortimer who was Earl of March. It was this Earl, rather than Hotspur's brother-in-law, whom Richard proclaimed heir to the English throne.

Shakespeare often transposes dates. The proposed Crusade is placed by Shakespeare shortly

after Henry IV's accession to the throne, whereas in fact it took place during the final year of his reign.

Shakespeare absents Owen Glendower and the Welsh Soldiery from the Battle of Shrewsbury, in order to further weaken the rebel cause and precipitate the victory of Henry IV, yet Holinshed states that the Welsh were present. Daniel disagrees, and Shakespeare follows Daniel (or took the lead himself for internally satisfying dramatic reasons).

Prince John, Hal's younger brother, is introduced by Shakespeare as a suitable foil or contrast to the Prince; yet historically Prince John must have been scarcely out of the cradle at this time.

Owen Glendower was probably not as visionary a Celt as he is made to seem by Shakespeare in this play, but Shakespeare seems to have based his character on that of the ancient magician, Merlin, in order to suit his plot. Besides, in this way Shakespeare further established the contrast between Glendower and his imaginativeness and caution, and Hotspur and his unimaginative, unreflecting impetuosity.

In the play the Prince refunded the money stolen by him from Falstaff, and by Falstaff from the stagecoach travelers, but not according to Stow's version.

According to Shakespeare King Henry IV was as generous to a defeated foe as he was towards the rebels, but according to history Hotspur's body was crushed between millstones and, afterwards, quartered.

In all these respects, Shakespeare is inaccurate historically; but all of the changes are justified in terms of playwrights' and poets' license.

THE LANGUAGE OF THE PLAY

Blank verse in iambic pentameter lines is spoken by the noble, serious characters in the play, while prose is employed by the ordinary low life characters. Prose occupies almost half the play. Scene ii of Act I is entirely in prose, except for the Prince's soliloquy at the end, which is in blank verse to mark the change of tone.

The Prince compares himself with the sun, and says that as it allows its true light to be concealed, so will he allow his true nature to be hidden; so that when at last it is revealed, it excites great wonder by the fact of having penetrated the clouds which appeared to envelop it. His reformation is established by several images ("like bright metal on a sullen ground") which emphasize the contrast between his present "loose behaviour" and his determination, later on, to "show more goodly and attract more eyes."

King Henry IV also speaks majestically in blank verse. Note how imperiously he addresses the rebellious and unsatisfactory Earl of Worcester, in Act V, Scene i.

Note how the "easy robes of peace" contrast with "ungentle steel" armor, and how civil war is described as "this churlish knot." Worcester's defection from the King's side causes him to be called "an exhaled meteor" and the King asks whether Worcester will go back to his "obedient orb again" where he formerly gave off "a fair and natural light." There is graciousness, pride, sorrow, strength and even wounded love in the King's voice as he speaks this verse.

Owen Glendower is a strange, elusive Celtic figure who believed that some divine significance was attached to his own birth. He expresses his boastfulness and egotism in verse of considerable splendor and power, full of references to magic and the occult. For this reason he appears as an eccentric and excitable Welshman to the sober and realistic, practical Hotspur.

The lines describing the crying of the herds are some of the best in the whole field of descriptive verse. Glendower's speech is thus full of strange signs and imagination.

Hotspur himself, though realistic and practical, was also hotheaded and, when upset, let his emotions run away with him. In Act I, Scene iii Hotspur is "drunk with choler" according to his father, the Earl of Northumberland, so much so that Worcester cannot tell him what he was planning to do until Hotspur has calmed down, several hundred lines later on.

As a vehicle to express the chivalry of knighthood and loyalty to the throne, the blank verse in this play is unsurpassed: while it serves to separate and mark off these honor-centered elements in the play from the humorous debauchery of Falstaff and his associates.

Bibliography

EDITIONS

A New Variorum Edition of Shakespeare, ed. Horace H. Furness. New York: J. B. Lippincott, 1871——. (Reprints by The American Scholar and Dover Publications.) Each play is dealt with in a separate volume of monumental scholarship.

The Yale Shakespeare, ed. Helge Kökeritz and Charles T. Prouty. New Haven: Yale University Press, 1955——. A multi-volume edition founded on modern scholarship.

COMMENTARY AND CRITICISM

Bentley, G. E. *Shakespeare and His Theatre.* Lincoln: University of Nebraska Press, 1964 (paperback). Illuminating discussion of the actual conditions under which, and for which, Shakespeare wrote.

Bradley, A. C. *Shakespearean Tragedy: Lectures on Hamlet, Othello, King Lear, Macbeth.* New York: Macmillan, 1904. (Paperback ed.; New York: Meridian Books, 1955.) A classic examination of the great tragedies.

Chambers, Edmund K. *William Shakespeare: A Study of Facts and Problems,* 2 vols. Oxford: Clarendon Press, 1930. Indispensable source for bibliographical and historical information.

Chute, Marchette. *Shakespeare of London.* New York: E. P. Dutton, 1949. A vivid account of Shakespeare's career in the dynamic Elizabethan metropolis.

Granville-Barker, Harley. *Prefaces to Shakespeare.* London: Sidgwick & Jackson, 1927-47. (2 vols.; Princeton: Princeton University Press, 1947.) Stimulating studies of ten plays by a scholarly man of the theater.

Harbage, Alfred. *Shakespeare's Audience.* New York: Columbia University Press, 1941. Revealing approach to Shakespeare as a practical man of the theater.

Knight, Wilson. *The Wheel of Fire.* London: Oxford University Press, 1930. Stresses the power of intuition to capture the total poetic experience of Shakespeare's work.

Spurgeon, Caroline. *Shakespeare's Imagery and What It Tells Us.* Cambridge: Cambridge University Press, 1935. A psychological study of the playwright's imagery as a means to understanding the man himself.

20

The History
of
King Henry IV, Part 1

Dramatis Personae

GROUP 1—THE ROYAL COURT
KING HENRY IV, formerly Henry Bolingbroke, Duke of Lancaster.
HENRY, PRINCE OF WALES, known as Prince Hal.
JOHN, PRINCE OF LANCASTER, Hal's younger brother and foil.
EARL OF WESTMORELAND.
SIR WALTER BLUNT.
Lords, Officers, Sheriff, and Attendants.

GROUP 2—The REBELS AND MEMBERS OF THE CONSPIRACY
THOMAS PERCY, EARL OF WORCESTER.
HENRY PERCY, EARL OF NORTHUMBERLAND.
HENRY PERCY surnamed Hotspur, his son.
EDMUND MORTIMER, EARL OF MARCH.
RICHARD SCROOP, ARCHBISHOP OF YORK.
ARCHIBALD, EARL OF DOUGLAS.
OWEN GLENDOWER.
SIR RICHARD VERNON.
LADY MORTIMER, daughter to Glendower, wife to Mortimer.
LADY PERCY, wife to Hotspur, sister to Mortimer.
SIR MICHAEL, friend to the Archbishop of York.

GROUP 3—THE CHARACTERS OF THE TAVERN
SIR JOHN FALSTAFF.
Poins.
Gadshill.
Peto.
Bardolph.
Mistress Quickly, Hostess of the Boar's Head Tavern in Eastcheap.
Vintner, Chamberlain, Drawers (Francis and Ralph),
two Carriers, Travelers.

22

HENRY IV, 1

ACT I SCENE I

The play opens in the royal palace in London. King Henry IV, his younger son (Prince John), and several senior courtiers are listening to the old and dignified king, who is making a speech about the serious situation in England at this time.

For the audience, the sight of these nobles in their robes of state with the Gothic architecture of the background presents a fine and colorful spectacle.

The king has been preparing to go on a Crusade to the Holy Land, but these preparations must be broken off because of fresh dangers at home.

"The irregular and wild Glendower," the leader of the Welsh forces, has defeated an English force sent to subdue them, and has taken the Earl of March (Mortimer) prisoner. Also Henry Percy, known as Hotspur, has put down a Scottish rebellion and taken some very important prisoners who, by the rules of war, should have been handed over to the king. But Hotspur refuses to transfer these prisoners, and Henry IV is worried by this act of arrogant disobedience.

The audience is interested to find out what is going to happen as a result of these domestic disturbances.

In the course of the scene Henry reveals another of his anxieties, concerning his other son's riotous conduct. He is envious of the Earl of Northumberland for having a son (Hotspur) who is "the theme of honour's tongue" in contrast to his own son and heir, Prince Hal the Prince of Wales), whose brow is stained (so the king believes) by "riot and dishonour."

Honor is one of the themes of this play, and it is interesting to see that Shakespeare pits Hotspur and Hal against one another from the beginning: they are of the same age (at least, in this play), on opposite sides, and one represents honor, the other dishonor. What will become of this, we wonder.

Westmoreland explains that Hotspur's defiance is prompted by "his uncle's teaching." This uncle is the Earl of Worcester, and he is "malevolent to you (Henry) in all aspects," i.e., wishes ill to the king for various reasons soon to be fully explained. Henry has sent for Worcester to come to the Council and explain his grievances. Until next Wednesday at Windsor Castle the king will plan what steps he has to take next.

ACT ONE, scene one.

(LONDON. THE PALACE.)

Enter KING HENRY, LORD JOHN OF LANCASTER, THE EARL OF WESTMORELAND, SIR WALTER BLUNT, *and* Others.

King. So shaken as we are, so wan with care,	1
Find we a time for frighted peace to pant,	2
And breathe short-winded accents of new broils	3
To be commenced in stronds afar remote.	4
No more the thirsty entrance of this soil	
Shall daub her lips with her own children's blood;	
No more shall trenching war channel her fields,	
Nor bruise her flowerets with the armed hoofs	8
Of hostile paces: those opposed eyes,	9
Which, like the meteors of a troubled heaven,	10
All of one nature, of one substance bred,	
Did lately meet in the intestine shock	12
And furious close of civil butchery	13
Shall now, in mutual well-beseeming ranks,	14
March all one way and be no more opposed	
Against acquaintance, kindred and allies:	
The edge of war, like an ill-sheathed knife,	17
No more shall cut his master. Therefore, friends,	18
As far as to the sepulchre of Christ,	19
Whose soldier now, under whose blessed cross	
We are impressed and engaged to fight,	21
Forthwith a power of English shall we levy;	22
To chase these pagans in those holy fields	23
Over whose acres walk'd those blessed feet	
Which fourteen hundred years ago were nail'd	
For our advantage on the bitter cross.	
But this our purpose now is twelve months old,	
And bootless 'tis to tell you we will go:	28
Therefore we meet not now. Then let me hear	
Of you, my gentle cousin Westmoreland,	
What yesternight our council did decree	
In forwarding this dear expedience.	32
Westmoreland. My liege, this haste was hot in question,	
And many limits of the charge set down	
But yesternight: when all athwart there came	35
A post from Wales loaden with heavy news;	36
Whose worst was, that the noble Mortimer,	
Leading the men of Herefordshire to fight	
Against the irregular and wild Glendower,	
Was by the rude hands of that Welshman taken,	40
A thousand of his people butchered;	
Upon whose dead corpse there was such misuse,	
Such beastly shameless transformation,	43
By those Welshwomen done as may not be	
Without much shame retold or spoken of.	
King. It seems then that the tidings of this broil	
Brake off our business for the Holy Land.	
Westmoreland. This match'd with other did, my	48
gracious lord;	
For more uneven and unwelcome news	

23

1. "wan": pale.

2. "peace to pant": metaphor (personification) expressing breathlessness of a peace which has been frightened away: relate to "breathe short-winded accents" in following line.

3. "broils": struggles.

4. "stronds": shores.

8. "flowerets": young men in the flower of their manhood.

9. "hostile paces": enemy footsteps (hoofs indicates horses' paces).

10. "meteors": signs of disaster to happen.

12. "intestine shock": literally internal; refers to domestic or internecine strife (suggests belly blows).

13. "furious close": strong language to reveal Henry's detestation of civil war.

14. "mutual well-beseeming ranks": more fittingly marching together against a common external foe than marching against one another.

17-18. "edge of war . . . cut his master": a metaphor and a simile to express the damage civil war does to all sides involved.

19. "sepulchre": tomb in the Holy Land in which Christ's body was laid prior to the resurrection. An object of pilgrimage by Christians (and Crusaders).

21. "impressed": pressed into (service) or conscripted.

22. "power of English": a force of soldiers.
"levy": We shall at once raise.

23. "pagans": Saracens here, though they were not pagan in the strict sense of the term, but Mohammedan.

28. "bootless": without fruit.

32. "expedience": expedition hastily undertaken.

35. "athwart": contrary to.

36. "post": messenger.
"heavy news": news of misfortune (transferred epithet).

40. "rude": rough and uncivilized.

43. "transformation": Welsh women were accused of committing atrocities on the corpses of the English dead.

48. "This matched . . . did": This unfortunate news accompanied by other bad tidings caused the Crusade to have been postponed.

HENRY IV, 1

ACT I SCENE I

The chief characters in the royal group have revealed some interesting and dramatically significant characteristics in this scene. The king is dignified and stern, concerned with affairs of state and able to take care of things as they develop; but we are also aware that he is "shaken" and "wan with care" already, and we know he is under considerable strain. The conflict between the king and his son and heir does not make the king's task easier.

The Earl of Westmoreland appears to be a wise and devoted counsellor, capable of explaining Hotspur's motives in terms of wily Worcester's ambitious discontent. There is no doubt about Westmoreland's loyalty.

Sir Walter Blunt is a devoted, loyal knight who performs valuable service as a royal messenger. It is Blunt who brings the news of the defeat of the Scottish Earl of Douglas by Hotspur at the recently held Battle of Holmedon. Hotspur's important prisoners included Mordake, Earl of Fife; the Earl of Athol; and the lords Murray, Angus, and Menteith.

We learn that Prince Hal is accused of riotous and disorderly conduct unbefitting the heir to the English throne, but we reserve judgment until we see the Prince on the stage: but our interest is aroused.

We learn of Owen Glendower, and speculate on what sort of wild Celt he will turn out to be. We hear of Hotspur's gallantry and look forward to seeing him on stage. We hear of the brave Scotsman (now prisoner), Archibald, Earl of Douglas. And we learn that the Earl of Worcester, an avowed enemy of Henry's, will soon be coming to court at Windsor to present his grievances.

This is a very successful opening scene since it introduces so many of the issues, conflicts, and characters in the play, and arouses the suspense of the audience by making us wonder what developments will take place. We are sure that there is going to be trouble.

Came from the north and thus it did import:
On Holy-rood day, the gallant Hotspur there,   51
Young Harry Percy and brave Archibald,
That ever-valiant and approved Scot,   53
At Holmedon met,   54
Where they did spend a sad and bloody hour;
As by discharge of their artillery,
And shape of likelihood, the news was told;
For he that brought them, in the very heat
And pride of their contention did take horse,   59
Uncertain of the issue any way.
  King. Here is a dear, a true industrious friend,
Sir Walter Blunt, new lighted from his horse,
Stained with the variation of each soil
Betwixt that Holmedon and this seat of ours;   64
And he hath brought us smooth and welcome news.
The Earl of Douglas is discomfited: 66
Ten thousand bold Scots, two and twenty knights,
Balk'd in their own blood did Sir Walter see   68
On Holmedon's plains. Of prisoners, Hotspur took
Mordake the Earl of Fife, and eldest son
To beaten Douglas; and the Earl of Athol,
Of Murray, Angus, and Menteith.
And is not this an honourable spoil?   73
A gallant prize? ha, cousin, is it not?
  Westmoreland. In faith,
It is a conquest for a prince to boast of.
  King. Yea, there thou makest me sad and makest
    me sin
In envy that my Lord Northumberland
Should be the father to so blest a son,
A son who is the theme of honour's tongue;
Amongst a grove, the very straightest plant;
Who is sweet Fortune's minion and her pride: 82
Whilst I, by looking on the praise of him,
See riot and dishonour stain the brow
Of my young Harry. O that it could be proved
That some night-tripping fairy had exchanged   86
In cradle-clothes our children where they lay,
And called mine Percy, his Plantagenet!   88
Then would I have his Harry, and he mine.
But let him from my thoughts. What think you, coz,   90
Of this young Percy's pride? the prisoners,
Which he in this adventure hath surprised,
To his own use he keeps; and sends me word,
I shall have none but Mordake Earl of Fife.
  Westmoreland. This is his uncle's teaching: this is
    Worcester,
Malevolent to you in all aspects;   96
Which makes him prune himself, and bristle up   97
The crest of youth against your dignity.   98
  King. But I have sent for him to answer this;
And for this cause awhile we must neglect
Our holy purpose to Jerusalem.
Cousin, on Wednesday next our council we
Will hold at Windsor, so inform the lords:
But come yourself with speed to us again;
For more is to be said and to be done
Than out of anger can be uttered.
  Westmoreland. I will, my liege.   [*Exeunt.*

51. "Holy-rood day": 14 September. Rood is an ancient word for cross (Heraclius recovered a piece of the true cross stolen by the King of Persia in 615 A.D., and this event is commemorated on this day).

53. "that ever-valiant and approved Scot": Note the favorable description of the Earl of Douglas.

54. "Holmedon": Near Wooler in the county of Northumberland, not far from the Scots border. Variously spelled Homildon etc. The battle actually took place here in September, 1402.

59. "contention": rival claim and struggle.

64. "seat": reference to the royal palace in London, one of the king's 'seats'.

66. "discomfited": defeated (literally put out of his comfort).

68. "Balk'd": piled up in balks or ridges (from an old northcountry term used in ploughing furrows).

73. "honourable spoil": SPOIL is reward gained in battle; so many titled prisoners could not but be honorable. Note the reference to the honor theme which recurs in this play.

82. "minion": darling (favorite).

86. "night-tripping fairy": it was commonly believed that elves and fairies sometimes exchanged well-favored babies for nasty ones who were often called changelings.

88. "Percy": the family name of the powerful family of the Earl of Northumberland.
"Plantagenet": the family name of the royal house of Anjou (France) to which Henry IV belonged.

90. "coz" affectionate abbreviation for cousin.

96. "Malevolent": full of evil will.

97-98. "bristle up/The crest of youth . . . .": a vivid image to express Hotspur's defiance of Henry IV. He is like a fighting cock bristling up his crest. Hotspur may even have worn a crested helmet.

HENRY IV, 1

ACT I SCENE II

In this scene members of the audience are introduced, for the first time in this play, to Sir John Falstaff and Prince Hal (the Prince of Wales and heir to the throne of England) in one of the royal apartments. They are talking light-heartedly about their tavern life and the risks of taking purses by night.

Prince Hal appears in a very favorable manner from the outset, despite what we had been led to expect of him from his father's bitter speech in the previous scene. Though consorting with thieves, he evidently does this out of an aristocratic taste for low life. And who could resist the opportunity to carouse with such a witty, lovable, lying rogue as Falstaff?

Scene two.

(LONDON. AN APARTMENT OF THE PRINCE'S.)

Enter THE PRINCE OF WALES *and* FALSTAFF.

Falstaff. Now, Hal, what time of day is it, lad?

Prince. Thou art so fat-witted, with drinking of old sack and unbuttoning thee after supper and sleeping upon benches after noon, that thou hast forgotten to demand that truly which thou wouldst truly know. What a devil hast thou to do with the time of day. Unless hours were cups of sack and minutes capons, and the blessed sun himself a fair wench in flame-colour'd taffeta, I see no reason why thou should'st be so superfluous to demand the time of day.

Falstaff. Indeed you come near me now, Hal; for we that take purses go by the moon and the seven stars, and not by Phoebus, he 'that wandering knight so fair.' And, I prithee, sweet wag, when thou art king, as, God save thy grace,—majesty I should say, for grace thou wilt have none,—

Prince. What, none?

Falstaff. No, by my troth, not so much as will serve to be prologue to an egg and butter.

Prince. Well, how then? come, roundly, roundly.

Falstaff. Marry, then, sweet wag, when thou art king, let not us that are squires of the night's body be called thieves of the day's beauty: let us be Diana's foresters, gentlemen of the shade, minions of the moon; and let men say we be men of good government, being governed, as the sea is, by our noble and chaste mistress the moon, under whose countenance we steal.

Prince. Thou sayest well, and it holds well too; for the fortune of us that are the moon's men doth ebb and flow like the sea, being governed, as the sea is, by the moon. As, for proof, now: a purse of gold most resolutely snatched on Monday night and most dissolutely spent on Tuesday morning; got with swearing 'Lay by' and spent with crying 'Bring in'; now in as low an ebb as the foot of the ladder and by and by in as high a flow as the ridge of the gallows.

Falstaff. By the Lord, thou sayest true, lad. And is not my hostess of the tavern a most sweet wench.

Prince. As the honey of Hybla, my old lad of the castle. And is not a buff jerkin a most sweet robe of durance?

Falstaff. How now, how now, mad wag! what, in thy quips and thy quiddities? what a plague have I to do with a buff jerkin?

Prince. Why, what a plague have I to do with my hostess of the tavern?

Falstaff. Well, thou hast called her to a reckoning many a time and oft.

Prince. Did I ever call for thee to pay thy part?

Falstaff. No; I'll give thee thy due, thou hast paid all there.

- 3
- 7
- 9
- 13
- 14
- 15
- 22
- 27
- 30
- 31
- 35
- 40
- 44

3. "sack": general name for a class of white wines formerly imported from Spain and the Canary Islands. Sherry, which also falls under this category, is still very popular in England, and is readily available from wooden casks stocked by better grocers.

7. "capons": specially fattened and castrated cock: much better eating than ordinary fowl.

9. "taffeta": lustrous kind of silk.

13. "Phoebus": Greek name for the sun (used humorously here).

14. "wag": witty fellow.

15. "grace": used in two senses as a pun: as a royal or ducal title, and in the sense of possessing the grace of God.

22. "squires of the night's body": pleasant-sounding names or euphemisms for highway-robbers.

27. "chaste mistress": oxymoron and pun on chased (which is what these "gentlemen of the shade" would be if they were detected at their favorite occupation by a troop of soldiers sent to track them down).

30-31. "ebb and flow": come in and out like the tides.

35. "Lay by": the cry of the highwayman to the driver of a stagecoach preparatory to stopping the coach by the side of the road; also contains a warning not to touch pistols.

40. "Hybla": town in Sicily well-known for its exquisite honey.
"old lad of the castle": a reference to Sir John Oldcastle which is what Falstaff was originally called. Oldcastle was a relative of the then Lord Chancellor, whose indignation caused Shakespeare to change the name. This reference was carelessly inserted in the first folio of 1623. Its humor is irrelevant today, but its irreverence would have appealed to Elizabethans who knew of Oldcastle's reputation.

44. "quips and thy quiddities": smart jokes and quibbles.

25

HENRY IV, 1

ACT I SCENE II

Falstaff knows the Prince enjoys tales of highwaymen or "gentlemen of the shade" but he believes that Hal will take action to stamp out highway robbery when he becomes king. The Prince says nothing to deny this, but does not let such serious considerations spoil the merriment of his meeting with Falstaff at this time. "Do not thou, when thou art king, hang a thief," pleads Falstaff, and the Prince jests wittily in reply.

The Prince, apparently, pays the reckoning (bill) at the Boar's Head Tavern in Eastcheap, and there is a passing discussion about this and Mistress Quickly, the hostess at that inn.

The manner in which Prince Hal takes up, extends, and completes some of Falstaff's comparisons, matching mood for mood in the most spontaneous give and take, demonstrates how much at ease the two are in one another's company. Yet Falstaff always seems to remember that he is with a future king of England, and tends to make frequent direct and indirect reference to this fact. Falstaff says "Thou hast the most unsavoury similes and are indeed the most comparative, rascalliest, sweet young prince."

Yet Falstaff knows the Prince is the object of much criticism by members of the royal court for the irresponsible company he keeps. "An old lord of the council rated me the other day in the street about you, sir, but I marked him not; and yet he talked very wisely, but I regarded him not..." The Prince neatly turns aside this reported criticism of his habits with a jest; but the remark has an effect upon him nevertheless.

As an escape from serious matters, Prince Hal asks where they should steal a purse of money tomorrow. Falstaff says wherever you want to, and promises to go along and take part. Yet earlier he had been talking of praying! "I see a good amendment of life in thee; from praying to purse-taking." This statement of the Prince's is humorously ironic, since Falstaff has not changed.

Poins, another high-spirited companion of the tavern group, enters, and, after some good-natured badinage relating to Fal-

Prince. Yea, and elsewhere, so far as my coin would stretch; and where it would not, I have used my credit.

Falstaff. Yea, and so used it that, were it not here apparent that thou art heir apparent—But, I prithee, sweet wag, shall there be gallows standing in England when thou art king? and resolution thus fobbed as it is with the rusty curb of old father antic the law? Do not thou, when thou art king, hang a thief.

Prince. No; thou shalt.

Falstaff. Shall I? O rare! By the Lord, I'll be a brave judge.

Prince. Thou judgest false already: I mean, thou shalt have the hanging of the thieves and so become a rare hangman.

Falstaff. Well, Hal, well; and in some sort it jumps with my humour as well as waiting in the court, I can tell you.

Prince. For obtaining of suits?

Falstaff. Yea, for obtaining of suits, whereof the hangman hath no lean wardrobe. 'Sblood, I am as melancholy as a gib cat or a lugged bear.

Prince. Or an old lion, or a lover's lute.

Falstaff. Yea, or the drone of a Lincolnshire bagpipe.

Prince. What sayest thou to a hare, or the melancholy of Moor-ditch?

Falstaff. Thou hast the most unsavoury similes and are indeed the most comparative, rascalliest, sweet young prince. But, Hal, I prithee, trouble me no more with vanity. I would to God thou and I knew where a commodity of good names were to be bought. An old lord of the council rated me the other day in the street about you, sir, but I marked him not; and yet he talked very wisely, but I regarded him not; and yet he talked wisely, and in the street too.

Prince. Thou didst well; for wisdom cries out in the streets, and no man regards it.

Falstaff. O, thou hast damnable iteration and art indeed able to corrupt a saint. Thou hast done much harm upon me, Hal; God forgive thee for it! Before I knew thee, Hal, I knew nothing; and now am I, if a man should speak truly, little better than one of the wicked. I must give over this life, and I will give it over: by the Lord, an I do not, I am a villain; I'll be damned for never a king's son in Christendom.

Prince. Where shall we take a purse to-morrow, Jack?

Falstaff. 'Zounds, where thou wilt lad; I'll make one; an I do not, call me a villain and baffle me.

Prince. I see a good amendment of life in thee; from praying to purse-taking.

Falstaff. Why, Hal, 'tis my vocation, Hal; 'tis no sin for a man to labour in his vocation.

Enter POINS.

Poins! Now shall we know if Gadshill have set a match. O! if men were to be saved by merit, what hole in hell were hot enough for him? This is the

57. "here apparent . . . heir apparent": an obvious pun.

60. "fobbed": cheated.

60-61. "old father antic the law": a delightful personification of the law which is often capricious and out of date, and so curbs or checks resolution.

72. "suits": lawsuits (see the pun with wardrobe).

75. "melancholy": The idea of Falstaff's being melancholy like a chained bear is laughable.

86. "rated": berated or told him off.

91-92. "wisdom cries out in the streets, and no man regards it": a humorous reference to the Old Testament (Proverbs 1, 20-24), Falstaff introduced this reference mockingly in lines 88-89.

93. "iteration": habit of repeating (in this case, the biblical quotation which Falstaff has just echoed). Notice how Falstaff poses as the injured saint for purpose of saying "and art indeed able to corrupt a saint." He pretends that Prince Hal has led him astray!

105. "amendment": change of heart and turning to better behavior.

107. "vocation" used ironically for the calling (of purse-taking).

HENRY IV, 1

ACT I SCENE II

staff's remorse for the life he leads and his inordinate liking for wines and meat ("Sir John Sack and Sugar" and "a cup of Madeira and a cold capon's leg"), informs them both that tomorrow morning at 4:00 a.m. at Gadshill a party of pilgrims will be traveling to Canterbury Cathedral, accompanied by merchants. All are carrying money. He outlines a plan for robbing these travelers, and has even ordered supper for the Prince and Falstaff tomorrow night at Eastcheap.

"We may do it [the robbery] as secure as sheep," declares Poins confidently, but the Prince refuses to accompany them. Falstaff and Poins plead with him to change his mind, but he seems adamant. Falstaff goes off to Eastcheap, leaving Poins and the Prince alone (which is exactly what Poins wanted).

Poins begins to cajole the Prince into taking part in the escapade because he (Poins) "has a jest to execute that he cannot manage alone." Falstaff, Bardolph, Peto, and Gadshill shall rob the travelers that Poins and the Prince have already waylaid; "yourself and I will not be there; and when they have the booty, if you and I do not rob them [i.e., the robbers], cut this head off from my shoulders" says Poins.

most omnipotent villain that ever cried 'Stand' to a true man.

Prince. Good morrow, Ned.

Poins. Good morrow, sweet Hal. What says Monsieur Remorse? what says Sir John Sack and Sugar? Jack! how agrees the devil and thee about thy soul, that thou soldest him on Good-Friday last for a cup of Madeira and a cold capon's leg?

Prince. Sir John stands to his word, the devil shall have his bargain; for he was never yet a breaker of proverbs; he will give the devil his due.

Poins. Then art thou damned for keeping thy word with the devil.

Prince. Else he had been damned for cozening the devil.

Poins. But, my lads, my lads, to-morrow morning by four o'clock, early at Gadshill! there are pilgrims going to Canterbury with rich offerings, and traders riding to London with fat purses: I have vizards for you all; you have horses for yourselves: Gadshill lies to-night in Rochester: I have bespoke supper to-morrow night in Eastcheap: we may do it as secure as sleep. If you will go, I will stuff your purses full of crowns; if you will not, tarry at home and be hanged.

Falstaff. Hear ye, Yedward; if I tarry at home and go not, I'll hang you for going.

Poins. You will, chops?

Falstaff. Hal, wilt thou make one?

Prince. Who, I rob? I a thief? not I, by my faith.

Falstaff. There's neither honesty, manhood, nor good fellowship in thee, nor thou camest not of the blood royal, if thou darest not stand for ten shillings.

Prince. Well then, once in my days I'll be a madcap.

Falstaff. Why, that's well said.

Prince. Well, come what will, I'll tarry at home.

Falstaff. By the Lord, I'll be a traitor then, when thou art king.

Prince. I care not.

Poins. Sir John, I prithee, leave the prince and me alone: I will lay him down such reasons for this adventure that he shall go.

Falstaff. Well, God give thee the spirit of persuasion and him the ears of profiting, that what thou speakest may move and what he hears may be believed, that the true prince may, for recreation sake, prove a false thief; for the poor abuses of the time want countenance. Farewell: you shall find me in Eastcheap.

Prince. Farewell, thou latter spring! farewell, All-hallow summer!

[Exit Falstaff.

Poins. Now, my good sweet honey lord, ride with us to-morrow: I have a jest to execute that I cannot manage alone. Falstaff, Bardolph, Peto and Gadshill shall rob those men that we have already waylaid; yourself and I will not be there; and when they have the booty, if you and I do not rob them, cut this head off from my shoulders.

112

116

128

130

135

137

162

167

112. "Stand" the notorious cry of the highwayrobber, usually followed by 'and deliver.'

116. "Monsieur Remorse": Poins has the intelligence to perceive that remorse was probably at the root of Falstaff's melancholy.

128. "Gadshill": both a place (here) and a thief (later). The coincidence is confusing, and is probably an error.

130. "vizards": masks for the face or the visors (eye-shields) of helmets, used for disguise here rather than protection.

135. "crowns": five shilling pieces (there is still a coin in use in Britain called the half-crown and worth two shillings and sixpence). Owing to devaluation, crowns would have bought considerably more when Shakespeare wrote than they do today. It is impossible to state the equivalent value in dollars with any certitude.

137. "Yedward": an affectionate, high-spirited version of Edward.

162. "thou latter spring . . . All hallow summer": Falstaff engages in the sports of youth though he is old; All Saints Day falls on 1 November, like Indian Summer (a false summer that precedes winter).

167. "Gadshill": one of the thieves (not to be confused with the place located between London and Rochester, on the road to Canterbury).

HENRY IV, 1

ACT I SCENE II

Prince Hal questions Poins in some detail about his plans for robbing the robbers of their booty, then says "Well, I'll go with thee: provide us all things necessary and meet me tomorrow night in Eastcheap; there I'll sup."

Shakespeare could have closed this scene there, but he wished to give the audience some insight into the deeper reaches of Hal's character. Therefore he gives the Prince the important soliloquy commencing:

I know you all, and will awhile uphold
The unyoked humour of your idleness:

Note that this soliloquy is in blank verse, in contrast to the remainder of the scene which is in prose. In this, Hal says, he will "imitate the sun,/Who doth permit the base contagious clouds/TO SMOTHER UP HIS BEAUTY FROM THE WORLD . . ." So Falstaff, Poins, Bardolph, and Peto—the tavern companions of his drinking bouts—shall serve TO CONCEAL HAL'S TRUE CHARACTER.

Thus: . . . WHEN HE PLEASE AGAIN TO BE HIMSELF, BEING WANTED, HE MAY BE MORE WONDER'D AT, By breaking through the foul and ugly mists Of vapours that did SEEM to strangle him.

He concludes in the same vein: I'll so offend, to make offence a skill, Redeeming time when men think least I will.

Note the effective use of the solitary rhymed couplet to round off this scene, and give beauty and emphasis to this important character-revealing speech.

Prince. How shall we part with them in setting forth?

Poins. Why, we will set forth before or after them, and appoint them a place of meeting, wherein it is at our pleasure to fail, and then will they adventure upon the exploit themselves; which they shall have no sooner achieved, but we'll set upon them.

Prince. Yea, but 'tis like that they will know us by our horses, by our habits and by every other appointment, to be ourselves.

Poins. Tut! our horses they shall not see; I'll tie them in the wood; our vizards we will change after we leave them: and, sirrah, I have cases of buckram for the nonce, to immask our noted outward garments.

Prince. Yea, but I doubt they will be too hard for us.

Poins. Well, for two of them, I know them to be as true-bred cowards as ever turned back; and for the third, if he fight longer than he sees reason, I'll forswear arms. The virtue of this jest will be the incom- 190 prehensible lies that this same fat rogue will tell us 191 when we meet at supper: how thirty, at least, he fought with; what wards, what blows, what extremities he endured; and in the reproof of this lies the jest.

Prince. Well, I'll go with thee: provide us all things necessary and meet me to-morrow night in Eastcheap; there I'll sup. Farewell. 198

Poins. Farewell, my lord. [*Exit.*

Prince. I know you all, and will awhile uphold
The unyoked humour of your idleness:
Yet herein will I imitate the sun,
Who doth permit the base contagious clouds 203
To smother up his beauty from the world,
That, when he please again to be himself,
Being wanted, he may be more wonder'd at,
By breaking through the foul and ugly mists
Of vapours that did seem to strangle him.
If all the year were playing holidays,
To sport would be as tedious as to work;
But when they seldom come, they wish'd-for come,
And nothing pleaseth but rare accidents.
So, when this loose behaviour I throw off
And pay the debt I never promised,
By how much better than my word I am,
By so much shall I falsify men's hopes;
And like bright metal on a sullen ground,
My reformation, glittering o'er my fault,
Shall show more goodly and attract more eyes
Than that which hath no foil to set it off.
I'll so offend, to make offence a skill, 221
Redeeming time when men think least I will.

190. "virtue": the essence or chief point.

191. "fat rogue": Falstaff.

198. "Eastcheap": the market district at the north end of London Bridge.

203. "base contagious clouds": low-flying clouds (literally earth-touching) that harbor disease. Note the alliteration of the consonant C in Contagious Clouds.

221. "make offence a skill": skillfully turn my misdeeds into advantages when the right time comes.

We return to the royal palace, in London, to find King Henry IV in a fit of rage and indignation with Earl of Worcester and other members of the Percy family, who had come to present their grievances to the king by royal invitation. Neither side is in a conciliatory mood. The meeting soon becomes an open quarrel. Hotspur's brother-in-law, Mortimer, has a better claim to the throne than Henry Bolingbroke has, so Henry is glad that Mortimer has put himself in the position of being accused of being a traitor by marrying the daughter of the rebellious Welsh chieftain, Owen Glendower. King Richard II had privately expressed the desire before his death that Mortimer should suceed him to the throne.

The powerful Percies had indeed helped to place Henry Bolingbroke upon the throne, and Henry IV is both jealous of their influence, and fearful that they will now turn their influence against him and support Mortimer as the rightful candidate for the throne.

Henry is glad to have Mortimer safely imprisoned and out of the way in Wales, but the king's refusal to send ransom money to bail him out angers the Percies, and Hotspur (acting on his uncle Worcester's instructions) refuses to transfer his important Scottish prisoners to the king, to whom they ought to be transferred according to the traditions of war.

The discontent of the Percies breaks out into open rebellion. It is interesting to trace the development of the quarrel in this scene. Worcester clearly warns the king:

Our house, my sovereign liege,
little deserves
The scourge of greatness to be
used on it;
And that same greatness too
which our own hands
Have holp to make so portly.

Northumberland, head of the Percy family, is about to join in also when Henry IV says:

Worcester, get thee gone; for
I do see
Danger and disobedience in
thine eye . . .

When Worcester has swept out, to return to the north to organize effective opposition to the king, Henry turns to Northumberland, and shows his essential fairmindedness by letting him speak in defense of his son Hotspur's actions. Afterwards, Hotspur speaks for himself in the splendid speech beginning at line 29. The mockery

Scene three.

(LONDON. THE PALACE.)

Enter THE KING, NORTHUMBERLAND, WORCESTER, HOTSPUR, SIR WALTER BLUNT, *with* Others.

King. My blood hath been too cold and temperate,
Unapt to stir at these indignities,   2
And you have found me; for accordingly
You tread upon my patience: but be sure
I will from henceforth rather be myself,
Mighty and to be fear'd, than my condition;   6
Which hath been smooth as oil, soft as young down,
And therefore lost that title of respect
Which the proud soul ne'er pays but to the proud.
   Worcester. Our house, my sovereign liege, little
      deserves
The scourge of greatness to be used on it;   11
And that same greatness too which our own hands
Have holp to make so portly.   13
   Northumberland. My lord,—
   King. Worcester, get thee gone; for I do see
Danger and disobedience in thine eye:
O, sir, your presence is too bold and peremptory,
And majesty might never yet endure
The moody frontier of a servant brow.
You have good leave to leave us: when we need   20
Your use and counsel, we shall send for you.
                              [*Exit* WORCESTER.
You were about to speak.   [*To* NORTHUMBERLAND.
   Northumberland.   Yea, my good lord.
Those prisoners in your highness' name demanded,
Which Harry Percy here at Holmedon took,
Were, as he says, not with such strength denied
As is deliver'd to your majesty:
Either envy, therefore, or misprision   27
Is guilty of this fault and not my son.
   Hotspur. My liege, I did deny no prisoners.
But I remember, when the fight was done,
When I was dry with rage and extreme toil,
Breathless and faint, leaning upon my sword,
Came there a certain lord, neat and trimly dress'd,
Fresh as a bridegroom; and his chin new reap'd
Show'd like stubble-land at harvest-home;
He was perfumed like a milliner,
And 'twixt his finger and his thumb he held
A pouncet-box, which ever and anon   38
He gave his nose and took't away again;
Who therewith angry, when it next came there,
Took it in snuff; and still he smiled and talk'd,   41
And as the soldiers bore dead bodies by,
He call'd them untaught knaves, unmannerly,
To bring a slovenly unhandsome corse   44
Betwixt the wind and his nobility.   45
With many holiday and lady terms
He question'd me; amongst the rest, demanded
My prisoners in your majesty's behalf.

2. "Unapt": disinclined.

6. "my condition": my usual self.

11. "scourge of greatness": i.e., the scourge (literally a whip for inflicting punishment) which those in power are able to authorize.

13. "Have holp": obsolete form of have helped portly, weighty and important.

20. "good leave to leave us": a pun.

27. "misprision": misunderstanding or error of communication.

38. "pouncet-box": snuff box (from Latin pumex, pumice stone). Relate to line 41.

44. "corse": old word for corpse.

45. "Betwixt": between.

HENRY IV, 1

ACT I SCENE III

expressed by Hotspur, the man of action, for the visiting lord, a courtier

> neat and trimly dress'd,
> Fresh as a bridegroom . . .

is a masterly example of scornful irony. Hotspur was "dry with rage and extreme toil" from the fighting, in contrast to the lord whose chin new reap'd

> Showed like stubble-land at
>   harvest home;
> He was perfumed like a
>   milliner,
> And 'twixt his finger and his
>   thumb he held
> A pouncet-box, which ever and
>   anon
> He gave his nose and took't
>   away again . . .

Hotspur answered this lord "indirectly" and his indirect reply was relayed to the king as an arrogant refusal to hand over the prisoners. He pleads with the king, but in a manly way, not to let this report come between his love and "your high majesty," as he puts it.

Sir Walter Blunt supports Hotspur in this story, and says his words to the visiting lord on that occasion should be allowed to die and not be held against him. Henry replies:

> Why, yet he doth deny his
>   prisoners,
> But with proviso and exception,
> That we at our own charge shall
>   ransom straight
> His brother-in-law, the foolish
>   Mortimer . . .

He goes on to accuse Mortimer of having, by his action of marrying into the enemy, revolted. Hotspur flies off the handle when he hears the word revolted applied to his brother-in-law, who, he swears, "never did fall off . . . but by the chance of war." He refers to Mortimer's wounds earned on the River Severn's sedgy bank while fighting Glendower for "the best part of an hour."

I then, all smarting with my wounds being cold,
To be so pester'd with a popinjay,   50
Out of my grief and my impatience
Answer'd neglectingly I know not what,
He should, or he should not; for he made me mad
To see him shine so brisk and smell so sweet
And talk so like a waiting-gentlewoman
Of guns and drums and wounds—God save the
    mark—
And telling me the sovereign'st thing on earth
Was parmaceti for an inward bruise;   58
And that it was great pity, so it was,
This villainous salt-petre should be digg'd   60
Out of the bowels of the harmless earth,
Which many a good tall fellow had destroy'd
So cowardly; and but for these vile guns,
He would himself have been a soldier.
This bald unjointed chat of his, my lord,
I answer'd indirectly, as I said;
And I beseech you, let not his report
Come current for an accusation
Betwixt my love and your high majesty.

Blunt. The circumstance consider'd, good my lord,
Whate'er Lord Harry Percy then had said
To such a person and in such a place,
At such a time, with all the rest retold,
May reasonably die and never rise
To do him wrong or any way impeach   75
What then he said, so he unsay it now.

King. Why, yet he doth deny his prisoners,
But with proviso and exception,   78
That we at our own charge shall ransom straight
His brother-in-law, the foolish Mortimer;
Who, on my soul, hath wilfully betray'd
The lives of those that he did lead to fight
Against that great magician, damn'd Glendower,
Whose daughter, as we hear, the Earl of March
Hath lately married. Shall our coffers, then,   85
Be emptied to redeem a traitor home?
Shall we buy treason? and indent with fears,
When they have lost and forfeited themselves?
No, on the barren mountains let him starve;   89
For I shall never hold that man my friend
Whose tongue shall ask me for one penny cost
To ransom home revolted Mortimer.   92

Hotspur. Revolted Mortimer!
He never did fall off, my sovereign liege,   94
But by the chance of war; to prove that true
Needs no more but one tongue for all those wounds,
Those mouthed wounds, which valiantly he took,   97
When on the gentle Severn's sedgy bank,   98
In single opposition, hand to hand,
He did confound the best part of an hour
In changing hardiment with great Glendower: 101
Three times they breathed, and three times did they   102
    drink,
Upon agreement, of swift Severn's flood;
Who then, affrighted with their bloody looks,   104
Ran fearfully among the trembling reeds,
And hid his crisp head in the hollow bank

---

50. "popinjay": a parrot or, as here, a coxcomb.
Note the effect of scorn achieved by alliterating the p consonant in line 50.

58. "parmaceti": spermaceti (obtained from whales).

60. "salt-petre": nitre (villainous because used in explosives).

75. "impeach": question in an accusatory tone.

78. "proviso and exception": make qualifications to nullify the effect of a statement or promise.

85. "coffers": money-chests (emptied to provide a ransom).

89. "barren mountains": Welsh mountains.

92. "revolted": employed in two senses; Mortimer has revolted, and is, therefore, revolting (to the king).

94. "fall off": become a rebel or traitor.

97. "mouthed wounds": wounds gaping and red like mouths.

98. "Severn's sedgy bank": the River Severn rises in North Wales near Aberystwith and flows 210 miles NE, SE, south, and SW to the Bristol Channel. At places its banks are covered with coarse, rushlike or flaglike herbs. Sedgy is the adjective from sedge. Note the repetition of the sibilant—s to give the effect of roughness.

101. "hardiment": hard blows.

102. "drink": by accident (when they fell into the river). By agreement is ironic.

104. "Who then, affrighted": the river was frightened of their wounded appearance and ran fearfully . . . This figure of speech is called pathetic fallacy, in which nature (the river) is made (by Shakespeare) capable or responding (by running fearfully) to human emotions (the fighting Mortimer and Glendower). (It is a form of metaphysical conceit, and appeals because of its stretching and inverting of the truth in order to stress a point in an artistic manner). The basic metaphor is sustained for several lines by such words as head, colour, wounds.

HENRY IV, 1

ACT I SCENE III

To say that he revolted against Henry is a slanderous accusation (line 112). Henry denies that this heroic encounter ever took place, and orders Hotspur to hand over the Scottish prisoners without further delay, adding a threat: "or you will hear of it."

The king and his train exit, leaving an angry young Hotspur and an anxious father; Worcester enters, and evidently wishes to discuss matters of importance relating to the organization of the rebellion, but Hotspur's angry raving will not let either Worcester or Northumberland to speak a line.

Bloodstained with these valiant combatants.
Never did base and rotten policy
Colour her working with such deadly wounds;
Nor never could the noble Mortimer   110
Receive so many, and all willingly:
Then let not him be slander'd with revolt.   112
  King. Thou dost belie him, Percy, thou dost belie 113
    him;
He never did encounter with Glendower;
I tell thee,
He durst as well have met the devil alone
As Owen Glendower for an enemy.
Art thou not ashamed? But, sirrah, henceforth
Let me not hear you speak of Mortimer:
Send me your prisoners with the speediest means,
Or you shall hear in such a kind from me   121
As will displease you. My Lord Northumberland,
We license your departure with your son.
Send us your prisoners, or you will hear of it.
       [*Exeunt* KING HENRY, BLUNT, *and* Train.
  Hotspur. An if the devil come and roar for them,
I will not send them: I will after straight
And tell them so; for I will ease my heart,
Albeit I make a hazard of my head.
  Northumberland. What, drunk with choler? stay   129
    and pause awhile:
Here comes your uncle.
       Re-enter WORCESTER.
  Hotspur.   Speak of Mortimer!
'Zounds, I will speak of him; and let my soul   131
Want mercy, if I do not join with him:
Yea, on his part I'll empty all these veins,
And shed my dear blood drop by drop in the dust,
But I will lift the down-trod Mortimer
As high in the air as this unthankful king,
As this ingrate and canker'd Bolingbroke.   137
  Northumberland. Brother, the king hath made your
    nephew mad.
  Worcester. Who struck this heat up after I was
    gone?
  Hotspur. He will, forsooth, have all my prisoners;
And when I urged the ransom once again
Of my wife's brother, then his cheek look'd pale,
And on my face he turn'd an eye of death,
Trembling even at the name of Mortimer.
  Worcester. I cannot blame him: was not he pro-
    claim'd
By Richard, that dead is, the next of blood?   146
  Northumberland. He was; I heard the proclama-
    tion:
And then it was when the unhappy king,—
Whose wrongs in us God pardon!—did set forth
Upon his Irish expedition;
From whence he intercepted did return
To be deposed and shortly murdered.
  Worcester. And for whose death we in the world's
    wide mouth
Live scandalized and foully spoken of.
  Hotspur. But soft, I pray you; did King Richard
    then

110. "Nor never": a double negative which though ungrammatical today was emphatic in Elizabethan usage.

112. "slander'd": defamed by untruths told about him.

113. "belie him": tell a lie about him.

121. "such a kind": in such a manner.

129. "choler": blind unreasoning rage.

131. "'Zounds": an oath; corruption of by God's wounds.

137. "ingrate and canker'd Bolingbroke": ungrateful and diseased (but only from the point of view of the Percies).

146. "By Richard": A reference to Richard's proclamation that Mortimer was to succeed to the throne. This happened shortly before Richard left for the Irish Rebellion during which he was forced to return to England where he was deposed, imprisoned, and shortly afterwards murdered.

Proclaim my brother Edmund Mortimer
Heir to the crown?
   Northumberland.   He did; myself did hear it.
   Hotspur. Nay, then, I cannot blame his cousin
      king,
That wish'd him on the barren mountains starve.   159
But shall it be, that you, that set the crown
Upon the head of this forgetful man
And for his sake wear the detested blot
Of murderous subornation, shall it be,   163
That you a world of curses undergo,
Being the agents, or base second means,
The cords, the ladder, or the hangman rather?
O, pardon me, that I descend so low,
To show the line and the predicament
Wherein you range under his subtle king;
Shall it for shame be spoken in these days,
Or fill up chronicles in days to come,   171
That men of your nobility and power
Did gage them both in an unjust behalf   173
As both of you—God pardon it!—have done,
To put down Richard, that sweet lovely rose,
And plant this thorn, this canker, Bolingbroke?
And shall it in more shame be further spoken,
That you are fool'd, discarded and shook off
By him for whom these shames ye underwent?
No; yet time serves wherein ye may redeem
Your banish'd honours and restore yourselves
Into the good thoughts of the world again,
Revenge the jeering and disdain'd contempt
Of this proud king, who studies day and night
To answer all the debt he owes to you
Even with the bloody payment of your deaths:
Therefore, I say,—
   Worcester.   Peace, cousin, say no more:
And now I will unclasp a secret book,
And to your quick-conceiving discontents
I'll read you matter deep and dangerous,
As full of peril and adventurous spirit
As to o'er-walk a current roaring loud
On the unsteadfast footing of a spear.
   Hotspur. If he fall in, good-night! or sink or swim:
Send danger from the east unto the west,
So honour cross it from the north to south,   196
And let them grapple: O, the blood more stirs
To rouse a lion than to start a hare!
   Northumberland. Imagination of some great exploit
Drives him beyond the bounds of patience.
   Hotspur. By heaven, methinks it were an easy leap,
To pluck bright honour from the pale-faced moon,   202
Or drive into the bottom of the deep,
Where fathom-line could never touch the ground,
And pluck up drowned honour by the locks;
So he that doth redeem her thence might wear
Without corrival all her dignities:
But out upon this half-faced fellowship!
   Worcester. He apprehends a world of figures here,   209
But not the form of what he should attend.   210
Good cousin, give me audience for a while.
   Hotspur. I cry you mercy.

159. "on the barren mountains starve": now Hotspur understands exactly why Henry refuses to pay ransom for Mortimer, preferring him to starve.

163. "subornation": inciting somebody else to commit a crime, in this case treason and regicide.

171. "chronicles": records of the times.

173. "gage": to bind as by oath or promise; to pledge.

196. "So honour": Hotspur is so obsessed at this point that honor for him takes the form of getting even with the usurping Bolingbroke. He again refers to honor in line 202.

209-10. "He apprehends . . . attend": Worcester says that Hotspur sees with his imagination what he should do, but is not capable of paying attention to the practical details which are what he ought to be attending to.

HENRY IV, 1

ACT I SCENE III

Hotspur's tongue runs on, and on, and on. He refers later on to that "same sword and buckler Prince of Wales" and we detect a note of rivalry which stirs our interest. The foxy Earl of Worcester lets Hotspur have his head until he has done, and when Hotspur assures him that he has finished the tirade, Worcester ironically says:

Nay, if you have not, to it again;
We will stay your leisure.

Worcester tells Hotspur to release the Scottish prisoners without ransom, retaining only the Earl of Douglas' son for liaison with the Scots. Meanwhile, the Earl of Northumberland is to creep into the favor of the Archbishop of York, who is only waiting a safe opportunity to rebel.

Hotspur's reaction to the plot is to approve it before he has heard all the details. Worcester

Worcester.   Those same noble Scots
That are your prisoners,—
Hotspur.   I'll keep them all;
By God, he shall not have a Scot of them;
No, if a Scot would save his soul, he shall not:
I'll keep them, by this hand.
Worcester.   You start away
And lend no ear unto my purposes.
Those prisoners you shall keep.
Hotspur.   Nay, I will; that's flat. 218
He said he would not ransom Mortimer;
Forbad my tongue to speak of Mortimer;
But I will find him when he lies asleep,
And in his ear I'll holla 'Mortimer!'
Nay,
I'll have a starling shall be taught to speak
Nothing but 'Mortimer', and give it him,
To keep his anger still in motion.
Worcester. Hear you, cousin; a word.
Hotspur. All studies here I solemnly defy,
Save how to gall and pinch this Bolingbroke:
And that same sword and buckler Prince of Wales, 230
But that I think his father loves him not
And would be glad he met with some mischance,
I would have him poison'd with a pot of ale.
Worcester. Farewell, kinsman: I'll talk to you
When you are better temper'd to attend.
Northumberland. Why, what a wasp-stung and impatient fool
Art thou to break into this woman's mood,
Tying thine ear to no tongue but thine own!
Hotspur. Why, look you, I am whipp'd and scourged
     with rods,
Nettled and stung with pismires, when I hear
Of this vile politician, Bolingbroke.
In Richard's time—what do you call the place?—242
A plague upon it, it is in Gloucestershire,
'Twas where the madcap duke his uncle kept,
His uncle York; where I first bow'd my knee
Unto this king of smiles, this Bolingbroke,—
'Sblood!—
When you and he came back from Ravenspurgh. 248
Northumberland. At Berkley castle.
Hotspur. You say true:
Why, what a candy deal of courtesy   251
This fawning greyhound then did proffer me!
Look, 'when his infant fortune came to age',
And, 'gentle Harry Percy', and 'kind cousin';
O, the devil take such cozeners! God forgive me! 255
Good uncle, tell your tale; I have done.
Worcester. Nay, if you have not, to it again;
We will stay your leisure.
Hotspur.   I have done, i' faith.
Worcester. Then once more to your Scottish prisoners.
Deliver them up without their ransom straight,
And make the Douglas' son your only mean
For powers in Scotland; which, for divers reasons
Which I shall send you written, be assured,

218. "that's flat": this downright and emphatic expression has become proverbial in English.

230. "sword and buckler": insulting because these weapons were used only by serving men and men of inferior rank and fortune.

242. "what . . . place?": Hotspur cannot remember the name of Berkley Castle, because he is so worked up!

248. "Ravenspurgh": a port on the east coast of Yorkshire that has long since disappeared inland owing to the silting process carried out by the local currents and the action of the River Humber. Henry Bolingbroke landed here on returning from exile.

251. "candy deal of courtesy": the sweet politeness with which Henry Bolingbroke treated Hotspur and the other Percies in order to win their support. Note the originality of the phrase, and the effective alliteration of the c consonant.

255. "cozeners": cheaters. Note the pun with calling kind cousin.

HENRY IV, 1

ACT I SCENE III

is confident of the success of the plan, which essentially involves combining the supporters of the Percies with the Scots forces and the Welsh forces against the army of Henry IV. Speed is necessary if, as Worcester punningly puts it, they are to "save their heads by raising of a head," i.e., a force of soldiers.

Worcester warns Hotspur not to take any action other than that decided upon already, and promises an early meeting probably in Wales. On this note of determined plotting, the scene closes.

The plot has been hatched; Hotspur has his instructions to send the noble Scottish prisoners (except one, Douglas' son) home without ransom, thereby seeking to earn their support. Worcester is going to gain Glendower's support (Mortimer has already married Glendower's daughter), and the Earl of Northumberland is to win the support of the influential Archbishop of York, who has no cause to love Henry IV. In theory at least it sounds like a formidable combination of forces against the king, and we wonder how he can possibly withstand their concerted efforts which, in any case, are leading once again to bloody civil strife.

However, Hotspur cannot refrain from expressing his impatient wish for a speedy ending of the conflict in a rhymed couplet that marks the cue for the curtain to drop.

Will easily be granted. You, my lord, [*To Northumberland.*
Your son in Scotland being thus employ'd,
Shall secretly into the bosom creep
Of that same noble prelate, well beloved,   267
The archbishop.
  Hotspur. Of York, is it not?
  Worcester. True; who bears hard
His brother's death at Bristol, the Lord Scroop.   271
I speak not this in estimation,
As what I think might be, but what I know
Is ruminated, plotted and set down,
And only stays but to behold the face
Of that occasion that shall bring it on.
  Hotspur. I smell it: upon my life, it will do well.
  Northumberland. Before the game is afoot, thou
    still let'st slip.
  Hotspur. Why, it cannot choose but be a noble plot:
And then the power of Scotland and of York,
To join with Mortimer, ha?
  Worcester.   And so they shall.
  Hotspur. In faith, it is exceedingly well aim'd.
  Worcester. And 'tis no little reason bids us speed,
To save our heads by raising of a head.
For, bear ourselves as even as we can,
The king will always think him in our debt,
And think we think ourselves unsatisfied,
Till he hath found a time to pay us home:
And see already how he doth begin
To make us strangers to his looks of love.
  Hotspur. He does, he does: we'll be revenged on him.
  Worcester. Cousin, farewell: no further go in this
Than I by letters shall direct your course.
When time is ripe, which will be suddenly,
I'll steal to Glendower and Lord Mortimer;
Where you and Douglas and our powers at once,
As I will fashion it, shall happily meet,
To bear our fortunes in our own strong arms,
Which now we hold at much uncertainty.
  Northumberland. Farewell, good brother: we shall
    thrive, I trust.
  Hotspur. Uncle, adieu: O, let the hours be short
Till fields and blows and groans applaud our sport!
                  [*Exeunt.*

267. "prelate": archbishop (in this case) of York.

271. "Lord Scroop": the archbishop's brother, had evidently died at Bristol. The archbishop was upset by his brother's death, and may have suspected Bolingbroke's orders were at least partly responsible. He is on the verge of rebelling, but awaits a safe opportunity.

Imagine for yourself an inn yard, in darkness; the only light comes from the carrier's lantern which glows fitfully. There is much shouting, and we dimly perceive horses and, occasionally, an ostler or groom. There is an atmosphere of carelessness and confusion. Although this is merely a short preparatory scene, it is good theater and fun when acted out on the stage.

Gadshill has an arrangement with one of the chamberlains at this inn whereby he will be told of any wealthy travelers who stay there, so that a fruitful robbery can be carried out. This arrangement was very common for an insider to pass information to the highwaymen.

ACT TWO, scene one.

(ROCHESTER. AN INN YARD.)

Enter a Carrier *with a lantern in his hand.*

First Carrier. Heigh-ho! an it be not four by the day I'll be hanged: Charles' wain is over the new chimney and yet our horse not packed. What, ostler!   2

Ostler. [*Within.*] Anon, anon.

First Carrier. I prithee, Tom, beat Cut's saddle, put a 5
few flocks in the point; poor jade, is wrung in the 6
withers out of all cess. 7

Enter another Carrier.

Second Carrier. Peas and beans are as dank here as 8
a dog, and that is the next way to give poor jades the
bots: this house is turned upside down since Robin 10
Ostler died.

First Carrier. Poor fellow, never joyed since the price 12
of oats rose; it was the death of him. 13

Second Carrier. I think this be the most villainous
house in all London road for fleas: I am stung like a
tench. 16

First Carrier. Like a tench! by the mass, there is
ne'er a king christen could be better bit than I have
been since the first cock. What, Ostler! come away
and be hanged! come away.

Second Carrier. I have a gammon of bacon and two
razes of ginger, to be delivered as far as charing- 22
cross. 23

First Carrier. God's body! the turkeys in my pannier 24
are quite starved. What, ostler! A plague on thee!
hast thou never an eye in thy head? canst not hear?
An't were not as good deed as drink, to break the
pate on thee I am a very villain. Come, and be
hanged! hast no faith in thee?

Enter GADSHILL.

Gadshill. Good morrow, carriers. What's o'clock?

First Carrier. I think it be two o'clock. 31

Gadshill. I prithee, lend me thy lantern, to see my
gelding in the stable.

First Carrier. Nay, by God, soft; I know a trick
worth two of that, i' faith.

Gadshill. I pray thee, lend me thine.

Second Carrier. Ay, when? canst tell? Lend me thy
lantern quoth he? marry, I'll see thee hanged first.

Gadshill. Sirrah carrier, what time do you mean to
come to London?

Second Carrier. Time enough to go to bed with a 42
candle, I warrant thee. Come, neighbour Mugs, we'll
call up the gentlemen: they will along with company, for they have great charge. [*Exeunt Carriers.*

Gadshill. What, ho! chamberlain.

Chamberlain. [*Within.*] At hand, quoth pick-purse.

Gadshill. That's even as fair as—at hand, quoth the
chamberlain; for thou variest no more from picking
of purses than giving direction doth from labouring;
thou layest the plot how.

2. "Charles' wain": seven bright stars in the constellation called the Great Bear. Wain means wagon.

5. "Cut's": common name for a work horse.

6. "flocks": pieces of wool for padding.
"point": sharp point of the saddle which needed padding to prevent abrasion.
"jade": sorry 'ill-conditioned' horse.

7. "withers": shoulder-blade ridge of a horse.
"cess": beyond calculation or ASSESSMENT.

8. "dank": humid (damp).

10. "bots": disease of horses caused by parasitic worms or maggots.

12. "joyed": enjoyed (his work).

13. "oats": probably a reference to the extremely high prices of grain and oats around 1596.

16. "tench": a fresh-water fish mistakenly believed to suffer from fleas.

22. "razes": roots (from Latin radix, root).

22-23. "Charing-cross": a district at the west end of the Strand, in London, England.

24. "pannier": wicker side basket(s) slung over the horse so as to hang down on either side in a balanced position.

31. "two o'clock": the First Carrier previously announced it was four o'clock (in line 1); besides being humorous, this wild inaccuracy reflects the rarity of time-pieces, even among the rich: poor serving men had to guess the time from the stars.

1704515

42. "Mugs": common name for a country bumpkin.

HENRY IV, 1

ACT II SCENE I

In this scene, after the colorful badinage of the first and second carriers, and the lazy ostler, the chamberlain informs Gadshill that the information previously given holds true still: a franklin (yeoman farmer) is carrying three hundred gold marks on his person; he was overheard telling this to a listener who is also well supplied with money.

A cheerful conversation about the hangman follows; hanging was the fate of most highway robbers who were unfortunate enough to be caught and convicted.

Gadshill then orders his horse, a gelding, to be brought from the stable, and rides off to the meeting place. We are all set for the robbery of the travelers, and we are armed with some interesting information that Gadshill lacks—namely, that Poins and Prince Hal have a little surprise up their sleeves for Gadshill's and Falstaff's group.

In this scene we meet many technical terms connected with horses and their care, and it will be necessary for you to refer often to the notes in the right hand column in order to follow exactly what is taking place. But do not attach undue importance to these terms; they add color and authenticity and are more important from the point of view of adding local color than from a structural dramatic point of view.

Incidentally, when Shakespeare lets the audience in on a secret which is not shared by certain other characters, he is employing the DRAMATIC device known as IRONY. We call it dramatic irony to distinguish it from all the other kinds of irony.

ACT II SCENE II

This is the scene in which two events for which we have already been prepared take place: the robbery of the travelers, first, and then the robbery of the robbers, second. The first lines convey the fact that Poins and Prince Hal

---

Enter CHAMBERLAIN.

Chamberlain. Good morrow, Master Gadshill. It holds current that I told you yesternight: there's a franklin in the wild of Kent hath brought three hundred marks with him in gold: I heard him tell it to one of his company last night at supper; a kind of auditor; one that hath abundance of charge too, God knows what. They are up already, and call for eggs and butter: they will away presently.

Gadshill. Sirrah, if they meet not with Saint Nicholas' clerks, I'll give thee this neck.

Chamberlain. No, I'll none of it: I pray thee, keep that for the hangman; for I know thou worshippest Saint Nicholas as truly as a man of falsehood may.

Gadshill. What talkest thou to me of the hangman? if I hang, I'll make a fat pair of gallows; for if I hang, old Sir John hangs with me, and thou knowest he is no starveling. Tut! there are other Trojans that thou dreamest not of, the which for sport sake are content to do the profession some grace; that would, if matters should be looked into, for their own credit sake, make all whole. I am joined with no foot-land rakers, no long-staff sixpenny strikers, none of these mad mustachio purple-hued malt-worms; but with nobility and tranquility, burgomasters and great-oneyers, such as can hold in, such as will strike sooner than speak, and speak sooner than drink, and drink sooner than pray; and yet 'zounds, I lie, for they pray continually to their saint, the commonwealth; or rather, not pray to her, but prey on her, for they ride up and down on her and make her their boots.

Chamberlain. What, the commonwealth their boots? will she hold out water in foul way?

Gadshill. She will, she will; justice hath liquored her. We steal as in a castle, cock-sure; we have the receipt of fern-seed, we walk invisible.

Chamberlain. Nay, by my faith, I think you are more beholding to the night than to fern-seed for your walking invisible.

Gadshill. Give me thy hand: thou shalt have a share in our purchase, as I am a true man.

Chamberlain. Nay, rather let me have it, as you are a false thief.

Gadshill. Go to; 'homo' is a common name to all men. Bid the ostler bring my gelding out of the stable. Farewell, you muddy knave. [*Exeunt.*

53
56

59
60

67

71
72
73

79

81

83
84
85
86

94

Scene two.

(THE HIGHWAY, NEAR GADSHILL.)

Enter PRINCE HENRY *and* POINS.

Poins. Come, shelter, shelter: I have removed Falstaff's horse, and he frets like a gummed velvet.

Prince. Stand close.

2

---

53. "franklin": yeoman farmer or holder of the freehold to a property. These men were in effect landed gentry.
"wild": the Weald or Wold of Kent (the south downs).

56. "auditor": official of the royal Treasury (as opposed to one who listens).
"charge": responsibility.

59-60. "St. Nicholas": patron saint of robbers.
"clerks": euphemism for highwaymen.

67. "Trojans": epic name used satirically for heroes.

71-72. "foot-land rakers": wandering footpads (thieves).

72. "long-staff sixpenny strikers": thieves bearing long staffs who are willing to knock down a victim for the sake of a small reward (sixpence).

73. "purple-hued malt-worm": purple-faced beer-drinkers.

79. "pray . . . prey": play upon words that sound the same but have different meanings (homophones).

81. "boots": booty (reward). Pun.

83. "foul way": when the roads were bad (as, in the sixteenth century, they usually were, especially after rain).

84-85. "justice hath liquored her": the poor manner in which justice is enforced makes crime (especially highway robbery) COMMON in the STATE (commonWEALTH); to liquor boots was to grease them to make them waterproof. It is a complex joke at several different levels.

86. "fern-seed: a plant popularly but mistakenly believed to make persons who took it invisible.

94. "homo": the generic name for man (homo sapiens).

2. "frets": a play on two meanings of this word (1) is vexed (2) frays or wears and tears easily.

have the upper hand from the start. Poins begins by robbing the fat Falstaff of his horse, thus forcing Sir John to walk—which is a form of locomotion he detests.

Falstaff complains loudly about having to walk because Poins has taken his horse, and this amuses us because Falstaff is breathless owing to his fatness, but this does not prevent his blowing off steam in this manner. Yet he has always found Poins a very pleasant drinking companion, or is it a love-potion that makes him like this rogue? "I'll starve 'ere I'll rob a foot further," he vows. Starve is one of the last things Falstaff would do.

The Prince warns them to listen in case the travelers should be approaching, and tells them all to lie down in order to do so: Falstaff asks "Have you any levers to lift me up again, being down?" which is a further reference to his great weight. He asks plaintively what they mean, to colt him thus, meaning to deceive him thus, and Prince Hal says you are not colted (deceived); you are un-colted (unhorsed), which is a neat pun.

Falstaff has the impudence to ask the Prince to help him find his horse, but the Prince refuses to act as his groom or horse-servant.

Falstaff is, indeed, much put out by the theft of his horse and even threatens to "split" on his colleagues in crime if, owing to his loss of mobility, he should be captured.

Bardolph and Gadshill arrive and confirm that lots of money is coming down the hill in a stage-coach destined for the royal treasury. Falstaff expresses the wish that it will go to the king's tavern instead.

Prince Hal cleverly dissociates himself from the other thieves, by sending Bardolph, Gadshill, Peto, and Falstaff on ahead to the narrow part of the lane where the "encounter" (line 61) is to take place. He and Poins are to stand guard.

Gadshill says there are eight or ten travelers and guards coming, and Falstaff displays some nervousness that they will rob him. He is accused of cowardice, and admits he is not another Duke of Lancaster (Hal's grandfather, noted for his bravery).

Enter FALSTAFF.

Falstaff. Poins! Poins, and be hanged! Poins!

Prince. Peace, ye fat-kidneyed rascal! what a brawling dost thou keep!

Falstaff. Where's Poins, Hal?

Prince. He is walked up to the top of the hill: I'll go seek him.

Falstaff. I am accursed to rob in that thief's company: the rascal hath removed my horse, and tied him I know not where. If I travel four foot by the squier further afoot I shall break my wind. Well, I doubt not but to die a fair death for all this, if I 'scape hanging for killing that rogue. I have forsworn his company hourly any time this two and twenty years, and yet I am bewitched with the rogue's company. If the rascal have not given me medicines to make me love him, I'll be hanged; it could not be else; I have drunk medicines. Poins! Hal! a plague upon you both! Bardolph! Peto! I'll starve ere I'll rob a foot further. An 'twere not as good a deed as drink, to turn true man and to leave these rogues, I am the veriest varlet that ever chewed with a tooth. Eight yards of uneven ground is threescore and ten miles afoot with me; and the stony-hearted villains know it well enough: a plague upon it when thieves cannot be true to one another! [*They whistle.*] Whew! A plague upon you all! Give me my horse, you rogues; give me my horse, and be hanged.

Prince. Peace! lie down; lay thine ear close to the ground and list if thou canst hear the tread of travellers.

Falstaff. Have you any levers to lift me up again, being down? 'Sblood, I'll not bear mine own flesh so far afoot again for all the coin in thy father's exchequer. What a plague mean ye to colt me thus.

Prince. Thou liest; thou art not colted, thou art un-colted.

Falstaff. I prithee, good Prince Hal, help me to my horse, good king's son.

Prince. Out, ye rogue! shall I be your ostler?

Falstaff. Go, hang thyself in thine own heir-apparent garters. If I be ta'en, I'll peach for this. An I have not ballads made on you all and sung to filthy tunes, let a cup of sack be my poison: when a jest is so forward, and afoot too! I hate it.

Enter GADSHILL, BARDOLPH *and* PETO *with him.*

Gadshill. Stand.

Falstaff. So I do, against my will.

Poins. O, 'tis our setter, I know his voice. Bardolph, what news?

Bardolph. Case ye, case ye; on with your vizards: there's money of the king's coming down the hill; 'tis going to the king's exchequer.

Falstaff. You lie, you rogue; 'tis going to the king's tavern.

Gadshill. There is enough to make us all.

Falstaff. To be hanged.

Prince. Sirs, you four shall front them in the narrow lane; Ned Poins and I will walk lower: if they 'scape from your encounter, then they light on us.

10

13

18

34

37

38

42

43
44
45

48

50

52

54

59

61

10. "that thief's": Poins'.

13. "squier": carpenter's set square.

18. "medicines": love potions.

34. "levers": humorous means of lifting a fat man to his feet (note that Falstaff employs his wit against himself frequently).

37. "colt": make a fool of or deceive.

38. "uncolted": unhorsed (or dehorsed).

42. "shall I . . .": Prince Hal rebuffs Falstaff's request which would turn him into acting as Sir John's horse-servant.

43. "heir-apparent": next in line to the throne.

44. "garters": the Order of the Garter is a decoration shared among the senior nobility.
"peach": (= impeach) accuse by informing on, hence 'slit on'.

45. "ballads": satirical verses set to music for singing in the streets.

48. "Stand": Falstaff is standing — against his will!

50. "setter": a hunting dog used to spy out the quarry: here it means Gadshill.

52. "vizards": masks.

54. "king's exchequer": the royal treasury.

59. "front": confront or face.

61. "light": alight upon.

HENRY IV, 1

ACT II SCENE II

Poins tells him that his horse stands behind the hedge, and leaves him "standing fast" (another pun, since Falstaff cannot move fast without a horse).

The Prince and Poins go away together to put on their disguises. Falstaff is urging on the others as the travelers enter, having just alighted from the stage-coach to lighten its load while going downhill. Carriage brakes in Elizabethan days were notoriously unreliable.

Shouting obstreperously, Falstaff makes the travelers stand and deliver their money, after which the other thieves bind them and leave. Prince Hal and Poins enter, see what has taken place, and stand close while the thieves return.

At the exact moment that Falstaff accuses the Prince and Poins of being cowards, they move in, in disguise, and set upon Falstaff and his company of thieves. They all run away, leaving the money which they had been on the point of sharing among themselves lying on the ground.

Hal takes charge of this money (about three hundred marks) and sums up the fray in a brief line that has gone into common English speech. They ride off thinking of Falstaff sweating his way home on foot. "How the rogue roar'd!"

Peto. How many be there of them? 62

Gadshill. Some eight or ten.

Falstaff. Zounds, will they not rob us?

Prince. What, a coward, Sir John Paunch?

Falstaff. Indeed, I am not John of Gaunt, your 66 grandfather, but yet no coward, Hal.

Prince. Well, we leave that to the proof.

Poins. Sirrah Jack, thy horse stands behind the hedge: when thou needest him, there thou shalt find him. Farewell, and stand fast.

Falstaff. Now cannot I strike him, if I should be hanged.

Prince. Ned, where are our disguises.

Poins. Here, hard by: stand close.

[*Exeunt Prince and Poins.*

Falstaff. Now, my masters, happy man be his dole, 76 say I: every man to his business.

Enter the Travellers.

First Traveller. Come, neighbor: the boy shall lead our horses down the hill; we'll walk afoot awhile, and ease our legs.

Thieves. Stand!

Travellers. Jesus bless us!

Falstaff. Strike; down with them; cut the villains' throats: ah! caterpillars! bacon-fed knaves! they hate us youth: down with them: fleece them. 85

Travellers. O, we are undone, both we and ours forever!

Falstaff. Hang ye, knaves, are ye undone? No, ye fat chuffs; I would your store were here! On, bacons, on! What, ye knaves! young men must live. You are grandjurors, are ye? we'll jure ye, 'faith.

[*Here they rob them and bind them. Exeunt.*

Re-enter PRINCE HENRY and POINS.

Prince. The thieves have bound the true men. Now could thou and I rob the thieves and go merrily to London, it would be argument for a week, laughter 94 for a month and a good jest for ever. 95

Poins. Stand close; I hear them coming.

Enter the Thieves again.

Falstaff. Come, my masters, let us share, and then to horse before day. An the Prince and Poins be not two arrant cowards, there's no equity stirring: there's 99 no more valour in that Poins than in a wild-duck.

Prince. Your money!

Poins. Villains!

[*As they are sharing, the Prince and Poins set upon them; they all run away; and Falstaff, after a blow or two, runs away too, leaving the booty behind them.*

Prince. Got with much ease. Now merrily to horse. 103
The thieves are all scatter'd and possess'd with fear
So strongly that they dare not meet each other;
Each takes his fellow for an officer.
Away, good Ned. Falstaff sweats to death,
And lards the lean earth as he walks along. 108
Were't not for laughing, I should pity him.

Poins. How the rogue roar'd! [*Exeunt.*

66. "Gaunt": the English form of Ghent (where Hal's grandfather, John o'Gaunt, came from). Note the pun on gaunt (= lean) and Paunch (= fat belly) on line 65.

76. "happy man be his dole": may every man be dealt out a portion of the reward from this robbery.

85. "youth" collective plural includes old Falstaff.

94-5. "argument . . . laughter . . . good jest": note how this sentence is structured to build up by gradations to a climax (week . . . month . . . for ever).

99. "equity": fair play.

103. "Got with much ease": This line has become a proverb.

108. "lards the lean earth": perspires into and thus greases the soil.

HENRY IV, 1

ACT II SCENE III

Hotspur is alone; he is reading a letter which has come to him at Warkworth Castle, the great family seat of the Percies in Northumberland. It is not clear who the letter is from, but the writer is evidently shrewd and cautious and sympathizes with the rebel cause, but refuses to associate himself with it formally for several good reasons.

These reasons are four, namely: 1) the undertaking is too dangerous; 2) the time is not ripe; 3) the allies are uncertain and 4) the king's forces are stronger than the rebel forces. Therefore, the writer advises against going on with the plot. Hotspur is enraged by this cautious attitude and angry at the refusal.

He accuses the writer of being a "shallow cowardly hind," but it is really Hotspur's assessment of the situation which is shallow. We expect Hotspur to rant on, and he does so — for twenty more lines.

Kate (Viscountess Percy) enters, and Hotspur bluntly announces that he will be leaving within two hours. Kate then makes a sweet and kindly speech expressing wifely concern for her husband's health. She has obviously been worrying about him, but does not realize that there is to be a general meeting of all the rebel groups by the ninth of next month. The Percies, Mortimer, York, Glendower, and the Earl of Douglas are all to be there.

Hotspur has evidently not been well lately, and has been talking in his sleep using technical terms associated with battle. These terms are explained in the right hand column.

Scene three.

(WARKWORTH CASTLE.)

Enter HOTSPUR, *solus, reading a letter.*

Hotspur. 'But, for mine own part, my lord, I could be well contented to be there, in respect of the love I bear your house.' He could be contented: why is he not, then? In respect of the love he bears our house: he shows in this, he loves his own barn better than he loves our house. Let me see some more. '*The purpose you undertake is dangerous;*'—why, that's certain: 'tis dangerous to take a cold, to sleep, to drink; but I tell you, my lord fool, out of this nettle, danger, we pluck this flower, safety. '*The purpose you undertake is dangerous; the friends you have named uncertain; the time itself unsorted; and your whole* (12) *plot too light for the counterpoise of so great an op-* (13) *position.*' Say you so, say you so? I say unto you again, you are a shallow cowardly hind, and you lie. (15) What a lack-brain is this! By the Lord, our plot is a good plot as ever was laid; our friends true and constant: a good plot, good friends, and full of expectation; an excellent plot, very good friends. What a frosty-spirited rogue is this! Why, my lord of York commends the plot and the general course of the action. 'Zounds, an I were now by this rascal, I could brain him with his lady's fan. Is there not my father, my uncle and myself? lord Edmund Mortimer, my lord of York and Owen Glendower? is there not besides the Douglas? have I not all their letters to meet me in arms by the ninth of the next month? and are they not some of them set forward already? What a pagan rascal is this! an infidel! Ha! you shall see (29) now in very sincerity of fear and cold heart, will he to the king and lay open all our proceedings. O, I could divide myself and go to buffets, for moving (32) such a dish of skim milk with so honourable an action! Hang him! let him tell the king: we are prepared. I will set forward to-night.

Enter LADY PERCY.

How now, Kate! I must leave you within these two
   hours.
Lady. O, my good lord, why are you thus alone?
Tell me, sweet lord, what is't that takes from thee
Thy stomach, pleasure and thy golden sleep?
Why dost thou bend thine eyes upon the earth,
And start so often when thou sitt'st alone?
Why hast thou lost the fresh blood in thy cheeks;
And given my treasures and my rights of thee (43)
To thick-eyed musing and cursed melancholy?
In thy faint slumbers I by thee have watch'd,
And heard thee murmur tales of iron wars;
Speak terms of manage to thy bounding steed; (47)
Cry 'Courage! to the field!' And thou hast talk'd
Of sallies and retires, of trenches, tents, (49)

---

12. "unsorted": ill chosen.

13. "counterpoise": weight used to balance against another weight of equivalent heaviness.

15. "hind": female red deer after its third year.

29. "pagan . . . infidel": a topical reference during the period of the Crusades. This reference makes him sound like a Saracen (one who did not share his faith).

32. "buffets": fight himself.

43. "my rights of thee": her conjugal rights of Hotspur.

47. "manage": direction and management of a battle.

49. "sallies": advances.
"retires": retreats.

HENRY IV, 1

ACT II SCENE III

Kate demands to know what Hotspur is up to, but instead of answering her, he calls a servant and inquires about a crop-eared roan horse that Butler has brought over from the sheriff. He goes off to ride this new horse in the park, leaving a disconsolate wife.

Kate asks Hotspur if he has been listening to her, but he does not even hear her question. She wants to know what it is that "carries you away" only to receive the evasive and literal reply "my horse" which both irritates and amuses her (and us). She reveals what she suspects: that he is going to "line" (support) her brother Mortimer's "enterprise" (plot to seize the throne). Hotspur makes a facetious interruption and there follows a lover's tiff during which Kate threatens to break Hotspur's little finger if he does not answer "directly unto this question." This is too much for Hotspur who pushes her away and declares that this is no world for playing at dolls or kissing with lips; we must fight our battles and look after our own interests.

At this cavalier if not downright churlish outbreak Kate is hurt, but Hotspur relents not at all and merely invites her to watch him ride the new horse in the park, on condition that she question him no more, especially about his military plans and arrangements.

Of palisadoes, frontiers, parapets, 50
Of basilisks, of cannon, culverin, 51
Of prisoners' ransom and of soldiers slain,
And all the currents of a heady fight.
Thy spirit within thee hath been so at war
And thus hath so bestirr'd thee in thy sleep,
That beads of sweat have stood upon thy brow
Like bubbles in a late-disturbed stream;
And in thy face strange motions have appear'd,
Such as we see when men restrain their breath
On some great sudden hest. O, what portents are 60
    these?
Some heavy business hath my lord in hand,
And I must know it, else he loves me not.
  Hotspur. What, ho!

Enter Servant.

     Is Gilliams with the packet gone?
Servant. He is, my lord, an hour ago.
Hotspur. Hath Butler brought those horses from the
    sheriff?
Servant. One horse, my lord, he brought even now.
Hotspur. What horse? a roan, a crop-ear, is it not? 67
Servant. It is, my lord.
Hotspur.   That roan shall be my throne.
Well, I will back him straight: O Esperance! 69
Bid Butler lead him forth into the park. [*Exit servant.*
  Lady. But hear you, my lord.
  Hotspur. What say'st thou, my lady?
  Lady. What is it carries you away?
  Hotspur. Why, my horse, my love, my horse.
  Lady. Out, you mad-headed ape!
A weasel hath not such a deal of spleen 76
As you are toss'd with. In faith,
I'll know your business, Harry, that I will.
I fear my brother Mortimer doth stir
About his title, and hath sent for you 80
To line his enterprise: but if you go,— 81
  Hotspur. So far afoot, I shall be weary, love.
  Lady. Come, come, you paraquito, answer me 83
Directly unto this question that I ask:
In faith, I'll break thy little finger, Harry,
An if thou wilt not tell me all things true.
  Hotspur. Away,
Away, you trifler! Love! I love thee not,
I care not for thee, Kate: this is no world
To play with mammets and to tilt with lips: 90
We must have bloody noses and crack'd crowns,
And pass them current too. God's me, my horse!
What say'st thou, Kate? what wouldst thou have
    with me?
  Lady. Do you not love me? do you not, indeed?
Well, do not then; for since you love me not,
I will not love myself. Do you not love me?
Nay, tell me if you speak in jest or no.
  Hotspur. Come, wilt thou see me ride?
And when I am o' horseback, I will swear
I love thee infinitely. But hark you, Kate,
I must not have you henceforth question me
Whither I go, nor reason whereabout:

50. "palisadoes": rows of stakes placed for defensive reasons.
"frontiers": barriers.
"parapets": walls.

51. "basilisks": heavy gun (reminiscent of a mythological serpent).
"cannon": plural.
"culverin": long thin rifle.

60. "portents": signs or omens.

67. "roan": reddish horse flecked with white.

69. "Esperance": French word for Hope; the family motto of the Percies.

76. "spleen": fiery impetuosity.

80. "title": claim to the throne based on Richard II's expressed wish.

81. "line": assist and support.

83. "paraquito": parrot.

90. "mammets": dolls or puppets.
"tilt": kiss passionately (the image of taking opposite sides in a tournament and encountering one another violently).

HENRY IV, 1

ACT II SCENE III

There are sound military reasons why an army officer should divulge as little information to his wife as possible, and Hotspur was probably right not to let his wife know anything about his tactical and strategic involvements. However, he might have been more tactful in the way in which he withheld this information. He knows she will not utter what she does not know, and this blunt approach even to his wife is characteristic of him. But he promises her one thing which, to her, atones for everything else: he will take her with him wherever he goes. She is satisfied with this, though it may involve physical hardship since there were no motels in those days.

ACT II SCENE IV

At the Boar's Head Tavern, in Eastcheap, Prince Hal and his faithful lieutenant, Poins, laugh until they almost collapse at the results of the trick in which they are anticipating. Hal has been drinking with three or four ordinary fellows, or "loggerheads" as he calls them, and has got on good terms with the drawers of wine, so that he is able to call each one by his name. There are three aspects to this long and humorous scene, which we shall call the confusion of Francis, calling Falstaff's bluff, and the royal play acting.

Hal has been learning the language of drinking as spoken by commoners, and now shows off some of the technical terms he has picked up. He then invites Ned Poins to take part in a plan to confuse or befuddle one of the stupidest of the tapsters, a fellow called Francis. When acted out upon the stage this incident is comic, but to be really effective it needs to be exaggerated.

Whither I must, I must; and, to conclude,
This evening must I leave you, gentle Kate.
I know you wise, but yet no farther wise
Than Harry Percy's wife: constant you are,
But yet a woman: and for secrecy,
No lady closer; for I well believe   108
Thou wilt not utter what thou dost not know;
And so far will I trust thee, gentle Kate.
Lady. How! so far?
Hotspur. Not an inch further. But hark you, Kate: 112
Whither I go, thither shall you go too;
To-day will I set forth, to-morrow you.
Will this content you, Kate?   115
Lady.   It must of force.   [*Exeunt.*

Scene four.

(THE BOAR'S-HEAD TAVERN, EASTCHEAP.)

Enter the PRINCE *and* POINS.

Prince. Ned, prithee, come out of that fat room, and   1
lend me thy hand to laugh a little.
Poins. Where hast been, Hal?
Prince. With three or four loggerheads amongst   4
three or four score hogsheads. I have sounded the   5
very base-string of humility. Sirrah, I am sworn
brother to a leash of drawers; and can call them all   7
by their christen names, as Tom, Dick, and Francis.   8
They take it already upon their salvation, that though   9
I be but Prince of Wales, yet I am the king of cour-   10
tesy; and tell me flatly I am no proud Jack, like Falstaff, but a Corinthian, a lad of mettle, a good boy,   12
by the Lord, so they call me, and when I am king of
England I shall command all the good lads in Eastcheap. They call drinking deep, dyeing scarlet; and
when you breathe in your watering, they cry 'hem!'   16
and bid you play it off. To conclude, I am so good a
proficient in one quarter of an hour, that I can drink   18
with any tinker in his own language during my life.
I tell thee, Ned, thou hast lost much honour, that thou
wert not with me in this action. But, sweet Ned,—to
sweeten which name of Ned, I give thee this pennyworth of sugar, clapped even now into my hand by
an under-skinker, one that never spoke other English   24
in his life than 'Eight shillings and sixpence', and
'You are welcome', with this shrill addition, 'Anon,   26
anon, sir! Score a pint of bastard in the Half-moon',   27
or so. But, Ned, to drive away the time till Falstaff
come, I prithee do thou stand in some by-room, while
I question my puny drawer to what end he gave me
the sugar; and do thou never leave calling 'Francis',
that his tale to me may be nothing but 'Anon'. Step
aside, and I'll show thee a precedent.
Poins. Francis!
Prince. Thou art perfect.
Poins. Francis!   [*Exit* POINS.

---

108. "No lady closer": none more able to keep a secret.

112. "Not an inch further": this expression has become proverbial in the common speech of English-speaking people.

115. "content": pleased and satisfied.

1. "fat": probably vat.

4. "loggerheads": numbskulls.

5. "hogsheads": largest sized barrels made by the coopers.

7. "leash": collective noun taken from a pack of hounds on the leash; hence, a pack of hounds or (by extension) of drawers.

8. "christen": the Prince imitates the 'low' pronunciation of the tapsters, and the deliberate misspelling indicates the mispronunciation of these servants.

9-10. "though . . . yet": note the balanced construction.

12. "Corinthian": a pleasure-loving fellow (from the city of Corinth, which was notorious for its 'pleasure').

16. "breathe in your watering": probably means take breath when you drink; the idea is to finish the glass (of beer) without taking a breath.

18. "proficient": this adjective is here used as a noun; it is not so employed today.

24. "under-skinker": under-drawer.

26. "anon": at once.

27. "bastard": wine of common or undetermined origin.

HENRY IV, 1

ACT II SCENE IV

THE CONFUSION OF FRANCIS

Poins goes into the adjoining vat room, from which he calls loudly for Francis, who calls that he is coming, and asks his fellow drawer, Ralph, to look after the "Pomgarnet" room (a mispronunciation of Pomegranate room). However, Prince Hal detains Francis and engages him in a one-sided and utterly nonsensical conversation designed to baffle the poor fellow. Meanwhile Poins keeps calling even more insistently and loudly for Francis, so that the poor stupid fellow is in a state of conflict and confusion and cannot move one way or the other.

The nonsensical and hilarious conversation between Prince Hal and Francis continues to redoubled cries of "Francis" from Poins in the adjoining room. Hal refuses to release the stupid fellow, whose bafflement is complete.

When acting this part, Hal must seem serious to Francis while conveying to the audience the fact that he is really having him on. This can be done in a very amusing manner.

Finally the Prince pretends to send Francis back to his duty by asking him "dost thou not hear them call?" but as Francis moves away from the royal presence, both the Prince and Poins call him at the same time, and the poor baffled drawer is transfixed, not knowing whether to remain or which way to go. The Vintner then enters and sends him packing about his business.

Enter FRANCIS.

Francis. Anon, anon, sir. Look down into the Pomgarnet, Ralph. 37

Prince. Come hither, Francis.

Francis. My lord?

Prince. How long hast thou to serve, Francis? 41

Francis. Forsooth, five years, and as much as to—

Poins. [*Within.*] Francis!

Francis. Anon, anon, sir.

Prince. Five year! by'r lady, a long lease for the clinking of pewter. But, Francis, darest thou be so valiant as to play the coward with thy indenture and 47 show it a fair pair of heels and run from it?

Francis. O Lord, sir, I'll be sworn upon all the books in England, I could find in my heart.

Poins. [*Within.*] Francis!

Francis. Anon, sir.

Prince. How old art thou, Francis?

Francis. Let me see—about Michaelmas next I shall be—

Poins. [*Within.*] Francis!

Francis. Anon, sir. Pray stay a little, my lord.

Prince. Nay, but hark you, Francis: for the sugar thou gavest me, 'twas a pennyworth, was't not?

Francis. O Lord, I would it had been two!

Prince. I will give thee for it a thousand pound: ask me when thou wilt, and thou shalt have it.

Poins. [*Within.*] Francis!

Francis. Anon, anon.

Prince. Anon, Francis? No, Francis; but to-morrow, Francis; or Francis, o' Thursday; or indeed, Francis, when thou wilt. But Francis!

Francis. My lord?

Prince. Wilt thou rob this leathern jerkin, crystal-button, not-pated, agate-ring, puke-stocking, caddis-garter smooth-tongue, Spanish-pouch,—

Francis. O Lord, sir, who do you mean?

Prince. Why then, your brown bastard is your only drink; for look you, Francis, your white canvas doublet will sully: in Barbary, sir, it cannot come to so much.

Francis. What, sir?

Poins. [*Within.*] Francis!

Prince. Away, you rogue! dost thou not hear them call?

[*Here they both call him; the drawer stands amazed, not knowing which way to go.*

Enter VINTNER.

Vintner. What, standest thou still, and hearest such a calling? Look to the guests within. [*Exit* FRANCIS. 81 My lord, old Sir John, with half-a-dozen more, are at the door: shall I let them in?

Prince. Let alone awhile, and then open the door.

[*Exit Vintner.*] Poins!

Re-enter POINS.

Poins. Anon, anon, sir.

Prince. Sirrah, Falstaff and the rest of the thieves are at the door; shall we be merry?

37. "Pomgarnet": Pomegranate (name of a Room).

41. "to serve": Francis's apprenticeship in serving.

47. "indenture": deed of apprenticeship.

81. "Vintner": literally one who manufactures wine, but in this case the supervisor of the serving men; a manager.

Poins. As merry as crickets, my lad. But hark ye; what cunning match have you made with this jest of the drawer? come, what's the issue?

Prince. I am now of all humours that have showed themselves humours since the old days of goodman Adam to the pupil age of this present twelve o'clock at midnight. [*Re-enter* FRANCIS.] What's o'clock, Francis? 94

Francis. Anon, anon, sir. [*Exit.*

Prince. That ever this fellow should have fewer words than a parrot, and yet the son of a woman! His industry is up-stairs and down-stairs; his eloquence the parcel of a reckoning. I am not yet of Percy's mind, the Hotspur of the north; he that kills me some six or seven dozen of Scots at a breakfast, washes his hands, and says to his wife 'Fie upon this quiet life! I want work.' 'O my sweet Harry,' says she, 'how many hast thou killed today?' 'Give my roan horse a drench,' says he; and answers 'Some fourteen,' an hour after; 'a trifle, a trifle.' I prithee, call in Falstaff. I'll play Percy, and that huge brawn shall play Dame Mortimer, his wife. 'Rivo!' says the drunkard. Call in ribs, call in tallow. 112 113

Enter FALSTAFF, GADSHILL, BARDOLPH, *and* PETO; FRANCIS *following with wine.*

Poins. Welcome, Jack: where hast thou been?

Falstaff. A plague of all cowards, I say, and a vengeance too! marry, and amen! Give me a cup of sack, boy. Ere I lead this life long, I'll sew nether stocks and mend them and foot them too. A plague of all cowards! Give me a cup of sack, rogue. Is there no virtue extant? [*He drinks.*] 117 118

Prince. Didst thou ever see Titan kiss a dish of butter? pitiful-hearted Titan, that melted at the sweet tale of the sun's! if thou didst, then behold that compound. 121

Falstaff. You rogue, here's lime in this sack too: there is nothing but roguery to be found in villainous man: yet a coward is worse than a cup of sack with lime in it. A villainous coward! Go thy ways, old Jack; die when thou wilt, if manhood, good manhood, be not forgot upon the face of the earth, then am I a shotten herring. There live not three good men unhanged in England; and one of them is fat and grows old: God help the while! a bad world, I say. I would I were a weaver; I could sing psalms or any thing. A plague of all cowards, I say still. 125 131

Prince. How now, wool-sack! what mutter you?

Falstaff. A king's son! If I do not beat thee out of thy kingdom with a dagger of lath, and drive all thy subjects afore thee like a flock of wild-geese, I'll never wear hair on my face more. You Prince of Wales!

Prince. Why, you round man, what's the matter?

Falstaff. Are not you a coward? answer me to that: and Poins there?

Poins. 'Zounds, ye fat paunch, an ye call me coward, by the Lord, I'll stab thee.

Falstaff. I call thee coward! I'll see thee damned

CALLING FALSTAFF'S BLUFF

Now follows a speech in which Hal lampoons (or parodies) the character of Hotspur most deliciously. This parody reveals that Hal has made an accurate assessment of Hotspur's character, and further prepares us for the meeting between these two young men at a later stage in this play.

Sir John Falstaff and half-a-dozen more men are at the door of the tavern, and Prince Hal and Poins (who have been, like us, waiting for this moment) invite Falstaff in, calling him "ribs" or "tallow."

Falstaff makes a brave entrance, loudly cursing "all cowards" and making it clear to everybody there that this collective term is intended to include Prince Hal and Poins, who were not there to play their proper parts when they should have been, at Gadshill. He rambles on, in characteristic Falstaffian fashion, and insults the Prince's manhood and valor. Hal bides his time, and Sir John has no idea of the trap into which he is about to fall. We in the audience are fully in the know, however, and the dramatic irony leading to suspense is delicious.

Falstaff sneers at Hal: "You Prince of Wales!" The very idea, he implies. He accuses the Prince and Poins of having shown their backs, not their faces, when needed.

Falstaff claims he took a thousand pounds from the travelers,

94. "humours": here means moods.

112. "Rivo": exclamation used at drinking-bouts (perhaps of Spanish origin).

113. "ribs . . . tallow": a scornful reference to Falstaff's corpulence.

117-18. "nether stocks": foot stockings.

121. "Titan": the sun (a giant).

125. "lime": lime was introduced by dishonest inn-keepers or their servants to restore temporary sparkle to wine that had gone flat and stale. This practice was believed to lead to stones in the bladder.

131. "shotten herring": female herring after it has released all its eggs and therefore appears lean.

HENRY IV, 1

but that this sum was stolen from them, in turn, by "a hundred upon poor four of us." Note the exaggeration. He goes on to say that he personally fought with a dozen of them at half-sword (close quarters) for two long hours, and was injured—behold the evidence of his wounds.

Prince Hal, who has been quiet until this point, innocently asks Falstaff to tell what really happened at Gadshill. Gadshill mentions a dozen attackers, Falstaff ups this number to sixteen, and claims they bound them all. Note the internal and external contradictions in this fantastic tale. As they exaggerate and lie, the Prince leads them neatly along. The numbers mentioned rise rapidly like prices at a popular auction.

ere I call thee coward: but I would give a thousand pound I could run as fast as thou canst. You are straight enough in the shoulders, you care not who sees your back: call you that backing of your friends? A plague upon such backing! give me them that will face me. Give me a cup of sack: I am a rogue, if I drunk to-day.

Prince. O villain! thy lips are scarce wiped since thou drunkest last.

Falstaff. All's one for that. [*He drinks.*] A plague of all cowards, still say I.

Prince. What's the matter?

Falstaff. What's the matter! there be four of us here have ta'en a thousand pound this day morning.

Prince. Where is it, Jack? where is it?

Falstaff. Where is it! taken from us it is: a hundred upon poor four of us.

Prince. What, a hundred, man?

Falstaff. I am a rogue, if I were not a half-sword 166 with a dozen of them two hours together. I have 'scaped by miracle. I am eight times thrust through the doublet, four through the hose; my buckler cut 169 through and through; my sword hacked like a hand-saw—*ecce signum!* I never dealt better since I was 171 a man: all would not do. A plague of all cowards! Let them speak: if they speak more or less than truth; they are villains and the sons of darkness.

Prince. Speak, sirs: how was it?

Gadshill. We four set upon some dozen—

Falstaff. Sixteen at least, my lord.

Gadshill. And bound them.

Peto. No, no, they were not bound.

Falstaff. You rogue, they were bound, every man of them; or I am a Jew else, an Ebrew Jew. 181

Gadshill. As we were sharing, some six or seven fresh men set upon us—

Falstaff. And unbound the rest, and then come in the other.

Prince. What, fought you with them all?

Falstaff. All! I know not what you call all? but if I fought not with fifty of them, I am a bunch of radish: if there were not two or three and fifty upon poor old Jack, then am I no two-legged creature.

Prince. Pray God you have not murdered some of them.

Falstaff. Nay, that's past praying for: I have pep- 193 pered two of them; two I am sure I have paid, two rogues in buckram suits. I tell thee what, Hal, if I 195 tell thee a lie, spit in my face, call me horse. Thou knowest my old ward; here I lay, and thus I bore my point. Four rogues in buckram let drive at me—

Prince. What, four? thou saidst but two even now.

Falstaff. Four, Hal; I told thee four.

Poins. Ay, ay, he said four.

Falstaff. These four came all a-front, and mainly thrust at me. I made me no more ado but took all their seven points in my target, thus.

Prince. Seven? why, there were but four even now.

Falstaff. In buckram?

Poins. Ay, four, in buckram suits.

166. "at half-sword": close fighting.

169. "doublet": lined jacket.
"hose": either long stockings or close fitting knee-breeches.
"buckler": shield.

171. "ecco signum": Latin for behold the evidence.

181. "Ebrew": Hebrew.

193. "peppered": sprinkled with holes like a pepper pot's top.

195. "buckram": coarse linen stiffened with gum or paste; this description is figurative, and means they were stiff, starched, and stuck up in manner.

44

HENRY IV, 1

ACT II SCENE IV

Falstaff's tale continues to enlarge. Two soon jumps to eleven; he mentions three more "in Kendal green" but mentions that it was so dark "thou couldst not see thy hand." Here the Prince begins to prick this balloon of lies and fabrications: if it were so dark, he says, how could you know they were in Kendal green?

Falstaff is called various sanguinary names by the amused but also irritated Prince, to which Sir John retaliates with a list of names that leaves him virtually breathless. After this vituperative exchange, Hal recounts what actually happened in a brief and factual speech. His method of telling the plain, unvarnished truth contrasts with Falstaff's ornamental bluff.

Falstaff might have been expected to be ashamed at being so expertly exposed, but he is not. He claims he recognized Hal from the beginning, and thought it was not for him (Falstaff) to "kill the heir-aparent." He claims he knew the Prince "on instinct" thereby introducing the famous word with which he will always be associated. His intuition told him not to touch the true prince. It is an amazingly plausible fiction, but nobody was deceived by it.

Falstaff changes his position so quickly, so neatly, and so completely, and is so unabashed by what has happened, that one cannot help admiring the rogue and

Falstaff. Seven, by these hilts, or I am a villain else.

Prince. Prithee, let him alone; we shall have more anon.

Falstaff. Dost thou hear me. Hal?

Prince. Ay, and mark thee too, Jack.

Falstaff. Do so, for it is worth the listening to. These nine in buckram that I told thee of—

Prince. So, two more already.

Falstaff. Their points being broken,—   216

Poins. Down fell their hose.

Falstaff. Began to give me ground: but I followed me close, came in foot and hand; and with a thought seven of the eleven I paid.

Prince. O monstrous! eleven buckram men grown out of two!

Falstaff. But, as the devil would have it, three misbegottén knaves in Kendal green came at my back 224 and let drive at me; for it was so dark, Hal, that thou couldst not see thy hand.

Prince. These lies are like their father that begets them; gross as a mountain, open, palpable. Why, 228 thou not-pated fool, thou obscene, greasy tallow-keech—

Falstaff. What, art thou mad? art thou mad? is not the truth the truth?

Prince. Why, how couldst thou know these men in Kendal green, when it was so dark thou couldst not see thy hand? come, tell us your reason: what sayest thou to this?

Poins. Come, your reason, Jack, your reason.

Falstaff. What, upon compulsion? 'Zounds, an I were at the strappado, or all the racks in the world, 239 I would not tell you on compulsion. Give you a reason on compulsion! if reasons were as plentiful as blackberries, I would give no man a reason upon compulsion, I.

Prince. I'll be no longer guilty of this sin; this sanguine coward, this horseback-breaker, this huge hill of flesh,—

Falstaff. 'Sblood, you starveling, you eel-skin, you dried neat's tongue, you stock-fish! O for breath to utter what is like thee! you tailor's yard, you sheath, you bow-case, you vile standing-tuck,—

Prince. Well, breathe awhile, and then to it again: and when thou hast tired thyself in base comparisons, hear me speak but this.

Poins. Mark, Jack.

Prince. We two saw you four set on four and bound them, and were masters of their wealth. Mark now, how a plain tale shall put you down. Then did we two set on you four; and, with a word, out-faced you from your prize, and have it; yea, and can show it you here in the house: and, Falstaff, you carried yourself away as nimbly, with as quick dexterity, and roared for mercy and still run and roared, as ever I heard bull-calf. What a slave art thou, to hack thy sword as thou hast done, and then say it was in fight! What trick, what device, what starting-hole, canst thou now find out to hide thee from this open and apparent shame?

216. "points": here used in a double sense to mean (1) tips of swords (2) braces, or suspenders used to keep up breeches.

224. "Kendal green": a kind of olive green woolen cloth manufactured at Kendal in Westmoreland and the surrounding district.

228. "palpable": capable of being touched.

239. "strappado": according to Holme's book ARMORY, "is when the person is drawn up to his height, and then suddenly to let him fall half way with a jerk, which not only breaketh his arms to pieces but shaketh all his joynts out of joynt."

ACT II SCENE IV

almost ends up believing him. He seems relieved at not having to invent any more lies, and is glad that the money is in Hal's safe-keeping (he takes this fact for granted).

Hal and Falstaff are reconciled and are about to settle down to drinking and extempore play-acting when Mistress Quickly enters to announce that a nobleman from the king is at the door with a message for the Prince. Sensing trouble, Hal is not at all anxious to see this messenger, especially since he has been carousing.

Falstaff goes out to send the grave old courtier packing.

During Falstaff's absence, Peto tells the Prince how Falstaff had hacked his own sword to make it appear that he had been fighting heavily, and had persuaded his men to do likewise. They had also pushed coarse grass up their noses to make them bleed, so that they could smeer the blood over their clothes to reinforce the impression they wished to make. When Falstaff comes in he does not realize that the cat is now completely out of the bag.

Poins. Come, let's hear Jack; what trick hast thou now?

Falstaff. By the Lord, I knew ye as well as he that made ye. Why, hear you, my masters: was it for me to kill the heir-apparent? should I turn upon the true prince? why, thou knowest I am as valiant as Hercules: but beware instinct; the lion will not 274 touch the true prince. Instinct is a great matter; I 275 was now a coward on instinct. I shall think the better of myself and thee during my life; I for a valiant lion, and thou for a true prince. But, by the Lord, lads, I am glad you have the money. Hostess, clap to the doors: watch to-night, pray to-morrow. Gallants, lads, boys, hearts of gold, all the titles of good fellowship come to you! What, shall we be merry? shall we have a play extempore? 283

Prince. Content; and the argument shall be thy running away.

Falstaff. Ah, no more of that, Hal, an thou lovest me.

Enter Hostess.

Hostess. O Jesu, my lord the prince!

Prince. How now, my lady the hostess! what sayest thou to me?

Hostess. Marry, my lord, there is a nobleman of the court at door would speak with you: he says he comes from your father.

Prince. Give him as much as will make him a royal man, and send him back again to my mother.

Falstaff. What manner of man is he?

Hostess. An old man.

Falstaff. What doth gravity out of his bed at midnight? Shall I give him his answer?

Prince. Prithee, do, Jack.

Falstaff. 'Faith, and I'll send him packing.   [*Exit.*

Prince. Now, sirs: by'r lady, you fought fair; so did you, Peto; so did you, Bardolph: you are lions too, you ran away upon instinct, you will not touch the true prince; no, fie!

Bardolph. 'Faith, I ran when I saw others run.

Prince. 'Faith, tell me now in earnest, how came Falstaff's sword so hacked?

Peto. Why, he hacked it with his dagger, and said he would swear truth out of England but he would make you believe it was done in fight, and persuaded us to do the like.

Bardolph. Yea, and to tickle our noses with spear- 313 grass to make them bleed, and then to beslubber our 314 garments with it and swear it was the blood of true men. I did that I did not this seven year before, I blushed to hear his monstrous devices.

Prince. O villain, thou stolest a cup of sack eighteen years ago, and wert taken with the manner, and ever since thou hast blushed extempore. Thou hadst fire and sword on thy side, and yet thou rannest away: what instinct hadst thou for it? 322

Bardolph. My lord, do you see these meteors? do 323 you behold these exhalations? 324

Prince. I do.

274. "Hercules": mythological strongman (see The labours of Hercules).

275. "Instinct": used in a special sense to mean intuitional as opposed to rational knowledge; a kind of sixth sense.

283. "extempore": unrehearsed (on the spur of the moment).

313. "spear-grass": coarse grass.

322. "instinct": a reference to Falstaff's previous use of this word as his excuse for not hurting the true prince.

323. "meteors": literally shooting stars; here used figuratively for facial carbuncles.

324. "exhalations": probably the fumes and sounds given off by Bardolph after having been through the emotional experience of confessing and drinking.

HENRY IV, 1

ACT II SCENE IV

Falstaff tells Hal that Sir John Bracy, the messenger from the court, has now left, but that Henry IV wishes to see Hal at the court tomorrow morning. Hal knows that his father's request is law, and that he must be there. Falstaff also reveals that the Percies of Northumberland, Owen Glendower of Wales, the Scottish Earl of Douglas, have all risen to support Mortimer against Henry IV; Mordake has joined the rebel side, and the wily Worcester has stolen away. The country is on the brink of civil war, and the situation is critical.

Bardolph. What think you they portend?
Prince. Hot livers and cold purses.   327
Bardolph. Choler, my lord, if rightly taken.   328
Prince. No, if rightly taken, halter.   329

Re-enter FALSTAFF.

Here comes lean Jack, here comes bare-bone. How 330
now, my sweet creature of bombast! How long is't
ago, Jack, since thou sawest thine own knee?
Falstaff. My own knee? when I was about thy years,
Hal, I was not an eagle's talon in the waist; I could
have crept into any alderman's thumb-ring: a plague
of sighing and grief! it blows a man up like a bladder. There's villainous news abroad: here was Sir
John Bracy from your father; you must to the court
in the morning. That same mad fellow of the north,
Percy, and he of Wales, that gave Amamon the bas- 340
tinado and swore the devil his true ligeman upon the 341
cross of a Welsh hook—what a plague call you him? 342
Poins. O, Glendower.
Falstaff. Owen, Owen, the same; and his son-in-law
Mortimer, and old Northumberland, and that
sprightly Scot of Scots, Douglas, that runs o' horse-
back up a hill perpendicular,—
Prince. He that rides at high speed and with his
pistol kills a sparrow flying. 349
Falstaff. You have hit it.
Prince. So did he never the sparrow.
Falstaff. Well, that rascal hath good mettle in him;
he will not run.
Prince. Why, what a rascal art thou then, to praise
him so for running!
Falstaff. O' horseback, ye cuckoo; but afoot he will
not budge a foot.
Prince. Yes, Jack, upon instinct.
Falstaff. I grant ye, upon instinct. Well, he is there
too, and one Mordake, and a thousand blue-caps
more: Worcester is stolen away to-night; thy father's
beard is turned white with the news: you may buy 362
land now as cheap as stinking mackerel. But tell 363
me, Hal, art not thou horrible afeard? thou being
heir-apparent, could the world pick thee out three
such enemies again as that fiend Douglas, that spirit
Percy, and the devil Glendower? Art thou not horribly afraid? doth not thy blood thrill at it?
Prince. Not a whit, i' faith; lack some of thy instinct.
Falstaff. Well, thou wilt be horribly chid to-morrow
when thou comest to thy father: if thou love me,
practise an answer.
Prince. Do thou stand for my father, and examine
me upon the particulars of my life.
Falstaff. Shall I? content: this chair shall be my
state, this dagger my sceptre, and this cushion my
crown.
Prince. Thy state is taken for a joint-stool, thy gold-
en sceptre for a leaden dagger, and thy precious
rich crown for a pitiful bald crown.
Falstaff. Well, an the fire of grace be not quite out
of thee, now shalt thou be moved. Give me a cup of

THE ROYAL PLAY-ACTING

Hal anticipated a stormy interview the following morning with his father, King Henry IV, and so to lighten his anxiety he agrees to enact the scene with Falstaff. A hilarious scene involving satire now follows, with Falstaff as Henry IV and Hal as himself (Prince of Wales). Falstaff assumes a tragic manner and rants in the vein of a Persian King, Cambyses, which is a parody of Preston's play. (See note on the right).

327. "hot livers and cold purses": empty purses after paying for the heating wine.

328-9. "Choler . . . halter": pun on collar and the hangman's noose. The whole play is full of references, mostly oaths or puns, to the act of hanging.

330. "lean Jack": another ironic refer- ence to Falstaff's corpulence.

340. "Amamon": name of a fiend (per- haps a corruption of the Greek name Agamemnon).

340. "bastinado": thrashing or cudgel- ling.

342. "Welsh hook": a weapon made from a pruning hook attached to a long staff.

349. "pistol": an anachronism since pis- tols were not in use during Henry IV's reign.

362-3. "you may buy land now as cheap as stinking mackerel": an interesting reference to the economic fact that the price of land fell during civil wars because the conqueror con- fiscated the estates of members of the losing side. If one felt that one was on the losing side (and mem- bers of both sides often felt this) one would be anxious to sell one's property and convert real estate into gold, which could be hidden or exported to a safe depository.

HENRY IV, 1

ACT II SCENE IV

Falstaff makes a speech in the manner of Henry IV, in which he mingles fatherly grief, righteous indignation, rebukes, and suitably balanced sentences; nor does he neglect to put in a powerful defense of himself, Falstaff. Note the flattering description he gives of himself.

Hal and Falstaff then reverse parts, and so the Prince plays his father the King.

sack to make my eyes look red, that it may be thought I have wept; for I must speak in passion, and I will do it in King Cambyses' vein. 386

Prince. Well, here is my leg.

Falstaff. And here is my speech. Stand aside, nobility.

Hostess. O Jesu, this is excellent sport, i' faith!

Falstaff. Weep not, sweet queen; for trickling tears are vain.

Hostess. O, the father, how he holds his countenance!

Falstaff. For God's sake, lords, convey my tristful queen; For tears do stop the flood-gates of her eyes.

Hostess. O Jesu, he doth it as like one of these players as ever I see!

Falstaff. Peace, good pint-pot; peace, good tickle-brain. Harry, I do not only marvel where thou spendest thy time but also how thou art accompanied: for though the camomile, the more it is trodden on the faster it grows, yet youth, the more it is wasted the sooner it wears. That thou art my son, I have partly thy mother's word, partly my own opinion, but chiefly a villainous trick of thine eye and a foolish hanging of thy nether lip, that doth warrant me. If then thou be son to me, here lies the point; why, being son to me, art thou so pointed at? Shall the blessed sun of heaven prove a micher and eat 410 blackberries? a question not to be asked. Shall the son of England prove a thief and take purses? a question to be asked. There is a thing, Harry, which thou hast often heard of and it is known to many in our land by the name of pitch: this pitch, as ancient writers do report, doth defile; so doth the company thou keepest: for, Harry, now I do not speak to thee in drink but in tears, not in pleasure but in passion, not in words only, but in woes also: and yet there is a virtuous man whom I have often noted in thy company, but I know not his name.

Prince. What manner of man, an it like your majesty?

Falstaff. A goodly portly man, i' faith, and a corpulent; of a cheerful look, a pleasing eye and a most noble carriage; and, as I think, his age some fifty, or, by'r lady inclining to three score; and now I remember me, his name is Falstaff; if that man should be lewdly given, he deceiveth me; for, Harry, I see virtue in his looks. If then the tree may be known by the fruit, as the fruit by the tree, then, peremptorily I speak it, there is virtue in that Falstaff: him keep with, the rest banish. And tell me now, thou naughty varlet, tell me, where hast thou been this month?

Prince. Dost thou speak like a king? Do thou stand for me, and I'll play my father.

Falstaff. Depose me? If thou dost it half so gravely, 437 so majestically, both in word and matter, hang me up by the heels for a rabbit-sucker or a poulter's hare.

Prince. Well, here I am set.

Falstaff. And here I stand: judge, my masters.

Prince. Now, Harry, whence come you?

Falstaff. My noble lord, from Eastcheap.

386. "King Cambyses' vein: in the ranting style of the character in the play, "a lamentable Tragedy, mix'd full of pleasant mirth," by Thomas Preston, dated 1569-70.

399. "Peace": this is an aside addressed to the Hostess, Mistress Quickly.

410. "micher": truant (our colloquial word moocher is derived from this).

437. "Depose": from playing the part of the king he has been deposed to play the part of the Prince.

48

HENRY IV, 1

ACT II SCENE IV

As Henry IV, Prince Hal begins the interrogation and soon launches into a vivid condemnation of Falstaff. Falstaff, as Hal, very adequately replies in his own defense. He claims that all Hal's other friends are false to him and deserve to be banished, but not "sweet," "kind," "true," "valiant," "old," and "plump," Jack Falstaff. He concludes movingly, "banish plump Jack, and banish all the world." Hal signifies his intention of doing just this!

This classic defense by Falstaff of himself is worth memorizing.

Bardolph runs in at this point to warn them that the sheriff and a large body of men (vigilantes, or watchmen) are at the gate and wish to search the inn. Everybody is alarmed, except the Prince, and Falstaff even talks of being hanged. Hal decides to receive the sheriff and all the others leave except Falstaff, who crawls behind the wall-hanging to listen in.

Prince. The complaints I hear of thee are grievous.

Falstaff. 'Sblood, my lord, they are false: nay, I'll tickle ye for a young prince, i'faith.

Prince. Swearest thou, ungracious boy? henceforth ne'er look on me. Thou are violently carried away from grace: there is a devil haunts thee in the likeness of an old fat man; a tun of man is thy companion. Why dost thou converse with that trunk of humours, that bolting-hutch of beastliness, that swollen parcel of dropsies, that huge bombard of sack, that stuffed cloak-bag, that roasted Manningtree ox, that reverend vice, that grey iniquity, that father ruffian, that vanity in years? Wherein is he good, but to taste sack and drink it? wherein neat and cleanly, but to carve a capon and eat it? wherein cunning, but in craft? wherein crafty, but in villainy? wherein villainous, but in all things? wherein worthy, but in nothing? 449 450 452 454 455

Falstaff. I would your grace would take me with you: whom means your grace?

Prince. That villainous abominable misleader of youth, Falstaff, that old white-bearded Satan.

Falstaff. My lord, the man I know.

Prince. I know thou dost.

Falstaff. But to say I know more harm in him than in myself, were to say more than I know. That he is old, the more the pity, his white hairs do witness it. If sack and sugar be a fault, God help the wicked! if to be old and merry be a sin, then many an old host that I know is damned: if to be fat be to be hated, then Pharaoh's lean kine are to be loved. No, my good lord; banish Peto, banish Bardolph, banish Poins: but for sweet Jack Falstaff, kind Jack Falstaff, true Jack Falstaff, valiant Jack Falstaff, and therefore more valiant, being, as he is, old Jack Falstaff, banish not him thy Harry's company, banish not him thy Harry's company: banish plump Jack, and banish all the world.

Prince. I do, I will.   [*A knocking heard.*

        [*Exeunt* Hostess, FRANCIS *and* BARDOLPH.

Re-enter BARDOLPH, *running.*

Bardolph. O, my lord, my lord! the sheriff with a most monstrous watch is at the door.

Falstaff. Out, ye rogue! Play out the play: I have much to say in the behalf of that Falstaff.

Re-enter the Hostess.

Hostess. O Jesu, my lord, my lord!

Prince. Heigh, heigh! the devil rides upon a fiddlestick: what's the matter?

Hostess. The sheriff and all the watch are at the door: they are come to search the house. Shall I let them in?

Falstaff. Dost thou hear, Hal? never call a true piece of gold a counterfeit: thou are essentially mad, without seeming so. 494

Prince. And thou a natural coward, without instinct.

Falstaff. I deny your major: if you will deny the sheriff, so; if not, let him enter: if I become not a 497

449-50. "devil . . . likeness": an unflattering description of Falstaff delivered by Prince Hal, and contrast it with that delivered by Falstaff himself in line 424 following.

450. "tun": cask for holding liquids (holds 252 gallons).

452. "humours": fluids.

454. "Manningtree ox": Manning-tree in Essex was noted for its roasted oxen at festival time.

455. "vice"; "iniquity": vanity: these might well have been printed with capital letters since they are the names of characters (personifications of various common sins) in the old morality plays.

494. "essentially mad": fundamentally insane because he lets the sheriff in.

497. "major": (pronounced mayor in the Latin way at this time), a term in logic to denote the first and most inclusive term in the syllogism, but here used also as a pun on sheriff since this officer was responsible to the mayor, as chief magistrate.

HENRY IV, 1

ACT II SCENE IV

The sheriff enters and courteously informs the Prince that he is searching for "a gross fat man" who has been seen to enter this inn. Hal promises that this man, whom he knows, will show up to-morrow to answer any charges that may be laid against him, and sends the sheriff off. The theft of a sum of three hundred, not one thousand marks has been mentioned in connecton with this fat man.

Hal goes to the arras to find Falstaff fast asleep and snoring like a porker.

While Falstaff snores they search his pockets, but find nothing interesting except itemized bills for meals eaten in tavern restaurants. Hal comments on the high proportion of wine to bread on these bills.

Hal has to go to court the next day, and the thought worries him. They must all go to the wars and play their proper parts in the battle that is going to divide the land. In order to get Falstaff to Shrewsbury, Hal promises to obtain for him a charge of foot (a commission in the infantry). He relishes the fact (so do we) that route-marches, which are a feature of infantry life, will be the death of him. He promises that the stolen money shall be repaid with interest, and bids Peto farewell.

cart as well as another man, a plague on my bringing up! I hope I shall as soon be strangled with a halter as another.

Prince. Go hide thee behind the arras: the rest walk 502 up above. Now, my masters, for a true face and good conscience.

Falstaff. Both which I have had: but their date is out, and therefore I'll hide me.

Prince. Call in the sheriff.

[*Exeunt all except the* PRINCE *and* PETO.

Enter Sheriff *and the* Carrier.

Now master sheriff, what is your will with me?

Sheriff. First, pardon me, my lord. A hue and cry 509
Hath follow'd certain men unto this house.

Prince. What men?

Sheriff. One of them is well known, my gracious
    lord,
A gross fat man.

Carrier.   As fat as butter.

Prince. The man, I do assure you, is not here;
For I myself at this time have employ'd him.
And, sheriff, I will engage my word to thee
That I will, by to-morrow dinner-time,
Send him to answer thee, or any man,
For any thing he shall be charged withal:
And so let me entreat you leave the house.

Sheriff. I will, my lord. There are two gentlemen
Have in this robbery lost three hundred marks.

Prince. It may be so: if he have robb'd these men,
He shall be answerable; and so farewell.

Sheriff. Good night, my noble lord.

Prince. I think it is good morrow, is it not?

Sheriff. Indeed, my lord, I think it be two o'clock.

[*Exeunt* Sheriff *and* Carrier.

Prince. This oily rascal is known as well as Paul's. 528
Go, call him forth.

Peto. Falstaff!—Fast asleep behind the arras, and snorting like a horse.

Prince. Hark, how hard he fetches breath. Search his pockets. [*He searcheth his pockets and findeth certain papers.*] What hast thou found?

Peto. Nothing but papers, my lord.

Prince. Let's see what they be: read them.

Peto. [*Reads*] Item, A capon,   2s. 2d.
        Item, Sauce,   4d.
        Item, Sack, two gallons,   5s. 8d.
        Item, Anchovies, and sack
          after supper   2s. 6d.
        Item, Bread,   ob.

Prince. O monstrous! but one half-pennyworth of bread to this intolerable deal of sack! What there is else, keep close; we'll read it at more advantage: there let him sleep till day. I'll to the court in the morning. We must all to the wars, and thy place shall be honourable. I'll procure this fat rogue a charge of foot; and I know his death will be a march 549 of twelve-score. The money shall be paid back with advantage. Be with me betimes in the morning; and so, good morrow, Peto. [*Exeunt.*

Peto. Good morrow, good my lord.

502. "arras": tapestry wall-hanging.

509. "hue and cry": hunting terms for shouting of alarm or protest (from the French verb huer, to shout).

528. "Paul's": St. Paul's Cathedral, in London, noted for its domed cupola (resembling Falstaff's belly). Falstaff is as well-known a landmark as St. Paul's is.

549. "charge of foot": commission roughly equivalent to a captaincy in the infantry (who fight on foot). Falstaff might well have preferred the cavalry who fought on horseback.

HENRY IV, 1

ACT III SCENE I

The Welsh meeting predicted earlier now takes place in the Archdeacon's house at Bangor, a small city in northern Caernarvonshire, Wales. The sympathy of many bishops is indicated by the loan of the church house to the rebels.

Mortimer is optimistic, but weak; Worcester is cunning and treacherous; Hotspur, brave but hot-headed and careless of details and planning preparations; Glendower is courteous, imaginative, self-centered, and somewhat boastful in a poetic way. It is not long before Hotspur clashes with Glendower, which bodes ill for the unity of their side at a time when disunity would be fatal.

Besides expressing his interesting and striking character, Glendower's speeches contain some of the best poetry in this play.

Glendower begins to boast about the fiery shapes that heralded his birth, and gives the impression his birth was of earth-shaking importance. This egotism grates on Hotspur and he tries to take him down a peg or two. Glendower tells him that he is a man who does not like being contradicted, and in effect warns him to be careful, but this advice is lost on Hotspur. Glendower again stresses that at his birth the front of heaven was full of fiery shapes, and declares that therefore he is not "in the roll of common men." This impresses everybody but Hotspur, and there is grave danger that the two men, so opposite in character yet united in the rebel cause, will break with one another openly in a quarrel. This is evidently what the others are also afraid of.

Glendower claims to be a master of the arts of magic, and second to none as a "deep experimenter." Hotspur makes a discourteous comment about Glendower's Welsh, and crudely makes as if to go off to dinner. Mortimer cautions him not to do so or he will make him mad (angry). Glendower boasts about his power to call spirits from the vasty deep, but Hotspur says anybody can do that, but will they come when called like this?

The two men waste time in this fruitless talk, and are obviously getting on one another's nerves when the mild Mortimer asks them to desist from this unprofitable chat.

Glendower continues to boast, this time about the number of times he has repulsed the English forces at the Welsh border. Three

---

ACT THREE, scene one.

(BANGOR. THE ARCHDEACON'S HOUSE.)

Enter HOTSPUR, WORCESTER, MORTIMER, *and* GLENDOWER.

Mortimer. These promises are fair, the parties sure, 1
And our induction full of prosperous hope. 2
Hotspur. Lord Mortimer, and cousin Glendower,
Will you sit down?
And uncle Worcester: a plague upon it!
I have forgot the map. 6
Glendower. No, here it is.
Sit, cousin Percy; sit, good cousin Hotspur,
For by that name as oft as Lancaster 8
Doth speak of you, his cheek looks pale and with
A rising sigh he wisheth you in heaven.
Hotspur. And you in hell as often as he hears
Owen Glendower spoke of.
Glendower. I cannot blame him: at my nativity 13
The front of heaven was full of fiery shapes,
Of burning cressets: and at my birth 15
The frame and huge foundation of the earth
Shaked like a coward.
Hotspur. Why, so it would have done at the same
season, if your mother's cat had but kittened, though
yourself had never been born.
Glendower. I say the earth did shake when I was
born.
Hotspur. And I say the earth was not of my mind,
If you suppose as fearing you it shook.
Glendower. The heavens were all on fire, the earth
did tremble.
Hotspur. O, then the earth shook to see the heavens
on fire,
And not in fear of your nativity.
Diseased nature oftentimes breaks forth
In strange eruptions; oft the teeming earth
Is with a kind of colic pinch'd and vex'd
By the imprisoning of unruly wind
Within her womb; which, for enlargement striving,
Shakes the old beldam earth and topples down 33
Steeples and moss-grown towers. At your birth
Our grandam earth, having this distemperature, 35
In passion shook.
Glendower. Cousin, of many men
I do not bear these crossings. Give me leave 37
To tell you once again that at my birth
The front of heaven was full of fiery shapes,
The goats ran from the mountains, and the herds
Were strangely clamorous to the frighted fields. 41
These signs have mark'd me extraordinary
And all the courses of my life do show
I am not in the roll of common men. 44
Where is he living, clipp'd in with the sea
That chides the banks of England, Scotland, Wales, 46
Which calls me pupil, or hath read to me?

---

1. "promises": made by rebel-sympathizers in different parts of the country, to send support.

2. "induction": being led in to claim the throne at the coronation.

6. "forgot the map": characteristic of Hotspur to forget such a vital piece of equipment in unfamiliar territory.

8. "Lancaster": Henry IV's family name from the dukedom of Lancaster.

13. "nativity": birth (a poetic word).

15. "cressets": open lamp or fire-basket set up to a beacon (used figuratively here).

33. "beldam": grandmother (note the sustained metaphor to describe earthquakes).

35. "distemperature": illness or other physical disorder.

37. "crossings": contradictions.

41. "clamorous": crying aloud. "frighted fields": transferred epithet.

44. "roll": book of names (used figuratively).

46. "chides": the angry vehemence and lashing of water.

HENRY IV, 1

ACT III SCENE I

times has he sent Henry's armies back where they came from. Hotspur even has a rude remark to make about this as though he were doubting Glendower's word. Glendower ignores this, and produces the map. They proceed to divide the land into three equal parts before they have even begun to conquer it, and the division is as follows: England, from the rivers Trent and Severn, is to go to Mortimer; Wales, from the river Severn, to Glendower; England and perhaps Scotland north of the river Trent, to Hotspur.

This tripartite division has been drawn up by the archdeacon of Bangor. The rebels plan to leave tomorrow to meet King Henry IV at Shrewsbury, where the battle will probably take place.

Suddenly Hotspur complains that his piece of land is not as large as the pieces allotted to the other leaders, because the river Trent curves up north and bites a large crescent out of his northern district. He talks wildly about damming up the river Trent and rerouting its course on a more even basis. Mortimer points out that the river also flows in a large crescent to the south, giving back to Hotspur as much land as it deprived him of, so that the balance is restored. Worcester says only a little rerouting trench is required, and Hotspur says he will have this trench dug, but then Glendower says he will not have the river's course changed. There follows a heated exchange during which Hotspur pours ridicule on Glendower's pronunciation of English only to hear the Welshman boast that he learned English at the royal court, and can play the harp and compose love songs in English, which is something he has never heard Hotspur doing.

And bring him out that is but woman's son
Can trace me in the tedious ways of art
And hold me pace in deep experiments. 50
 Hotspur. I think there's no man speaks better Welsh.
I'll to dinner.
 Mortimer. Peace, cousin Percy; you will make him mad.
 Glendower. I can call spirits from the vasty deep.
 Hotspur. Why, so can I, or so can any man;
But will they come when you do call for them?
 Glendower. Why, I can teach you, cousin, to command
The devil.
 Hotspur. And I can teach thee, coz to shame the 59
devil
By telling truth: to tell truth and shame the devil.
If thou have power to raise him, bring him hither,
And I'll be sworn I have power to shame him hence.
O, while you live, tell truth and shame the devil!
 Mortimer. Come, come, no more of this unprofitable chat.
 Glendower. Three times hath Henry Bolingbroke made head 65
Against my power; thrice from the banks of Wye
And sandy-bottom'd Severn have I sent him
Bootless home and weather-beaten back.
 Hotspur. Home without boots, and in foul weather too!
How 'scapes he agues, in the devil's name? 70
 Glendower. Come, here's the map: shall we divide our right
According to our threefold order ta'en?
 Mortimer. The archdeacon hath divided it
Into three limits very equally:
England, from Trent and Severn hitherto,
By south and east is to my part assign'd:
All westward, Wales beyond the Severn shore,
And all the fertile land within that bound,
To Owen Glendower: and, dear coz, to you
The remnant northward, lying off from Trent.
And our indentures tripartite are drawn; 81
Which being sealed interchangeably,
A business that this night may execute,
To-morrow, cousin Percy, you and I
And my good Lord of Worcester will set forth
To meet your father and the Scottish power,
As is appointed us, at Shrewsbury.
My father Glendower is not ready yet, 88
Nor shall we need his help these fourteen days.
Within that space you may have drawn together
Your tenants, friends and neighbouring gentlemen.
 Glendower. A shorter time shall send me to you, lords:
And in my conduct shall your ladies come:
From whom you now must steal and take no leave,
For there will be a world of water shed
Upon the parting of your wives and you.
 Hotspur. Methinks my moiety, north from Burton 97
here,

50. "experiments": magic.

59. "coz": an insulting familiarity here.

65. "made head": brought together an armed force for the purpose of attacking.

70. "agues": malarial fevers.

81. "indentures tripartite": contract drawn up in triplicate (by the Archdeacon).

88. "father": short for father-in-law.

97. "moiety": share or portion (not half, since more than two parts are involved).
"Burton": Burton-on Trent.

HENRY IV, 1

ACT III SCENE I

Hotspur retaliates with a blistering verbal attack on meter balladmongers and compares its forced gait (metrical regularity) to the forced gait of a shuffling nag.

Glendower then gives in, and permits Hotspur to change the course of the Trent, whereupon Hotspur gives up this fight saying he does not care about it any more.

Hotspur says he would give away three times as much land as the Trent seemed to deprive him of to any well-deserving friend, but when it comes to bargaining, he says, he would "cavil on the ninth part of a hair." Hotspur carelessly asks if the agreement has been drawn up, and without waiting for a reply wishes to be gone.

Glendower says it is a good night for traveling, and he will break the news of their departure to their wives. Glendower's daughter will take Mortimer's departure hard since she is very much in love with her recently married husband.

Mortimer rebukes Hotspur for provoking Glendower, Mortimer's

In quantity equals not one of yours:
See how this river comes me cranking in,
And cuts me from the best of all my land
A huge half-moon, a monstrous cantle out.   101
I'll have the current in this place damm'd up;
And here the smug and silver Trent shall run
In a new channel, fair and evenly;
It shall not wind with such a deep indent,
To rob me of so rich a bottom here.
   Glendower. Not wind? it shall, it must, you see it
     doth.
   Mortimer. Yea, but
Mark how he bears his course, and runs me up
With like advantage on the other side;
Gelding the opposed continent as much   111
As on the other side it takes from you.
   Worcester. Yea, but a little charge will trench him
     here
And on this north side win this cape of land;
And then he runs straight and even.
   Hotspur. I'll have it so: a little charge will do it.
   Glendower. I'll not have it alter'd.
   Hotspur.   Will not you?
   Glendower. No, nor you shall not.
   Hotspur.   Who shall say me nay?
   Glendower. Why, that will I.
   Hotspur. Let me not understand you, then; speak it
     in Welsh.
   Glendower. I can speak English, lord, as well as you;
For I was train'd up in the English court;
Where, being but young, I framed to the harp
Many an English ditty lovely well   124
And gave the tongue a helpful ornament,
A virtue that was never seen in you.   126
   Hotspur. Marry,
And I am glad of it with all my heart:
I had rather be a kitten and cry mew
Than one of these same metre ballad-mongers;   130
I had rather hear a brazen canstick turn'd,   131
Or a dry wheel grate on the axle-tree;   132
And that would set my teeth nothing on edge,
Nothing so much as mincing poetry:
'Tis like the forced gait of a shuffling nag.
   Glendower. Come, you shall have Trent turn'd.
   Hotspur. I do not care: I'll give thrice so much land
To any well-deserving friend;
But in the way of bargain, mark ye me,
I'll cavil on the ninth part of a hair.   140
Are the indentures drawn? shall we be gone?
   Glendower. The moon shines fair; you may away
     by night:
I'll haste the writer and withal
Break with your wives of your departure hence:
I am afraid my daughter will run mad,
So much she doteth on her Mortimer.   [*Exit.*
   Mortimer. Fie, cousin Percy! how you cross my
     father!
   Hotspur. I cannot choose: sometime he angers me
With telling me of the moldwarp and the ant,   149
Of the dreamer Merlin and his prophecies,   150

101. "cantle": lit., corner-piece or segment of a sphere.

111. "Gelding": depriving of an essential part.

124. "lovely well": a Welsh idiom.

126. "virtue": skill or art here.

130. "ballad-mongers": contemptuous term for ballad-makers.

131. "canstick": short form for candlestick (turned on a lathe, a noisy process).

132. "grate": scrape loudly.

140. "cavil": raise trivial objections.

149. "moldwarp": mole (the animal).

150. "Merlin": magician who aided King Arthur.

HENRY IV, 1

ACT III SCENE 1

father-in-law. Hotspur says he cannot help it, for all Glendower's boasting about magic practices and signs makes him angry and makes him lose faith in the Welsh leader's sagacity.

Mortimer attempts to explain to Hotspur that Glendower has many good qualities and that he is something of a scholar and experimenter. He is brave as a lion, and easy to get along with, and generous "as mines of India." He holds Hotspur's temper in high respect, and allows Hotspur to say things to him that he would hear from nobody else.

Worcester supports Mortimer in entreating Hotspur to be more careful in what he says to Glendower. He tells Hotspur that he is "too wilful-blame" and that he must learn to mend this fault. Wilfulness sometimes results from greatness, courage, breeding, but at other times it shows anger, lack of manners, bad government, pride, haughtiness, failure to consider the views of others, and scorn: and such bad qualities damage the noblemen who possess them.

Hotspur blithely agrees in a short two line speech that sounds almost like a rhymed couplet (except that speed does not rhyme with leave) when the ladies enter with Glendower.

Mortimer complains bitterly that "My wife can speak no English, I no Welsh." Glendower acts as an interpreter; Dame Mortimer weeps because she will not part with her husband; she wishes to be a soldier too, and go to the wars with her husband. Mortimer bids Glendower tell her that she and Aunt Percy (that is, Hotspur's wife, Kate,) will follow in their steps speedily. Glendower speaks to her about this in Welsh, and she answers in the same language and seems pleased at the news.

And of a dragon and a finless fish,
A clip-wing'd griffin and a moulten raven,　152
A couching lion and a ramping cat,　153
And such a deal of skimble-skamble stuff　154
As puts me from my faith. I tell you what;
He held me last night at least nine hours
In reckoning up the several devils' names
That were his lackeys; I cried 'hum,' and 'well, go to,'
But mark'd him not a word. O, he is as tedious
As a tired horse, a railing wife;　160
Worse than a smoky house: I had rather live
With cheese and garlic in a windmill, far,
Than feed on cates and have him talk to me　163
In any summer-house in Christendom.

Mortimer. In faith, he is a worthy gentleman,
Exceedingly well read, and profited
In strange concealments, valiant as a lion
And wondrous affable and as bountiful
As mines of India. Shall I tell you, cousin?
He holds your temper in high respect
And curbs himself even of his natural scope
When you come 'cross his humour; faith, he does:
I warrant you, that man is not alive
Might so have tempted him as you have done,
Without the taste of danger and reproof:
But do not use it oft, let me entreat you.

Worcester. In faith, my lord, you are too wilful-
　　blame;　177
And since your coming hither have done enough
To put him quite beside his patience.
You must needs learn, lord, to amend this fault:
Though sometimes it show greatness, courage,
　　blood—
And that's the dearest grace it renders you—
Yet oftentimes it doth present harsh rage,
Defect of manners, want of government,
Pride, haughtiness, opinion and disdain:
The least of which haunting a nobleman
Loseth men's hearts and leaves behind a stain
Upon the beauty of all parts besides,
Beguiling them of commendation.

Hotspur. Well, I am school'd: good manners be
　　your speed!　190
Here come our wives, and let us take our leave.

　　Re-enter GLENDOWER *with the* Ladies.

Mortimer. This is the deadly spite that angers me.
My wife can speak no English, I no Welsh.

Glendower. My daughter weeps: she will not part
　　with you;
She'll be a soldier too, she'll to the wars.

Mortimer. Good father, tell her that she and my
　　Aunt Percy　196
Shall follow in your conduct speedily.
　　　　[*Glendower speaks to her in Welsh,*
　　　　and she answers him in the same.

Glendower. She is desperate here; a peevish self-　198
　　willed thing,
That no persuasion can do good upon.
　　　　　　[*The lady speaks in Welsh.*

152. "griffin": mythical creature with the head, wings and forelegs of an eagle, and the body, hind legs, and tail of a lion.
"moulten": having moulted.

153. "couching": heraldic term for a lion lying down, as opposed to rampant, which means upright (as used to describe the shields of coats-of-arms).

154. "skimble-skamble stuff": confused, rambling nonsense.

160. "railing": nagging.

163. "cates": dainties, delicacies.

177. "wilful-blame": deliberately provoking, and to be blamed for being so.

190. "school'd": disciplined as by a schoolmaster.

196. "Aunt Percy": Kate (Hotspur's wife).

198. "peevish": cross, fretful, complaining.

HENRY IV, 1

ACT III SCENE I

Dame Mortimer speaks to her husband in Welsh and he understands her meaning from her looks. He is not only in love with the lady, but also with the Welsh language which she makes "as sweet as ditties highly penn'd" and sung by a fair queen to the music of the lute.

Dame Mortimer speaks again to him, in Welsh, and her father translates for Mortimer: she bids him lay down, on the rushes and rest his gentle head upon her lap, and she will sing him songs that please him, and make him sleep in an enchanted atmosphere. The speech is a very beautiful one, and is worth memorizing.

As the poetry develops, music is heard in the wings, and Glendower calls the musicians in to play while Mortimer and his lady, and Hotspur and Kate flirt with one another in their respective ways, Dame Mortimer delicately, and Kate rather more boisterously.

Kate is rebuked by Hotspur for not using strong language such as befits a great nobleman's wife; she apparently swears in a very middle-class manner which Hotspur does not consider strong enough. He says "Swear me, Kate, like a lady as thou art, a good mouth-filling oath . . ." and leave your other milk and mild expressions for "velvet-guards and Sunday-citizens."

Lady Percy will not sing, and Hotspur soon goes in to prepare for their departure which will take place in two hours. Glendower calls Mortimer, and tells him he is as slow to get ready as Lord Percy is on fire to go. Mortimer also goes out to get ready.

The plot is well under way, but with leaders like these we feel its chances of success are small.

Mortimer. I understand thy looks: that pretty Welsh
Which thou pour'st down from these swelling heavens
I am too perfect in; and, but for shame,
In such a parley should I answer thee.   203
          [*The lady speaks again in Welsh.*
I understand thy kisses and thou mine,
And that's a feeling disputation:
But I will never be a truant, love,
Till I have learn'd thy language; for thy tongue
Makes Welsh as sweet as ditties highly penn'd,   208
Sung by a fair queen in a summer's bower,
With ravishing division, to her lute.   210
    Glendower. Nay, if you melt, then will she run mad.
          [*The lady speaks again in Welsh.*
Mortimer. O, I am ignorance itself in this!
Glendower. She bids you on the rushes lay you
    down
And rest your gentle head upon her lap,
And she will sing the song that pleaseth you
And on your eyelids crown the god of sleep,
Charming your blood with pleasing heaviness,
Making such difference 'twixt wake and sleep
As is the difference betwixt day and night
The hour before the heavenly-harness'd team
Begins his golden progress in the east.
    Mortimer. With all my heart I'll sit and hear her
    sing:
By that time will our book, I think, be drawn.
    Glendower. Do so;
And those musicians that shall play to you
Hang in the air a thousand leagues from hence,
And straight they shall be here: sit, and attend.
    Hotspur. Come, Kate, thou art perfect in lying
down: come, quick, quick, that I may lay my head in   229
thy lap.
    Lady Percy. Go, ye giddy goose. [*The music plays.*
    Hotspur. Now I perceive the devil understands
    Welsh;
And 'tis no marvel he is so humorous.   233
By'r lady, he is a good musician.
    Lady Percy. Then should you be nothing but musi-
cal, for you are altogether governed by humours. Lie 236
still, ye thief, and hear the lady sing in Welsh.
    Hotspur. I had rather hear Lady, my brach, howl in
    Irish.
    Lady Percy. Wouldst thou have thy head broken?
    Hotspur. No.
    Lady Percy. Then be still.
    Hotspur. Neither; 'tis a woman's fault.
    Lady Percy. Now God help thee! What's that?
    Hotspur. Peace! she sings.
          [*Here the lady sings a Welsh song.*
    Hotspur. Come, Kate, I'll have your song too.
    Lady Percy. Not mine, in good sooth.
    Hotspur. Not yours, in good sooth! Heart! you
swear like a comfit-maker's wife. 'Not you, in good 248
sooth', and 'as true as I live', and 'as God shall mend
me', and 'as sure as day'.
And givest such sarcenet surety for thy oaths,   251
As if thou never walk'st further than Finsbury.   252

203. "parley": here means conversation or at any rate talking, if the meaning is not understood. Also used in the military sense elsewhere in this play.

208. "ditties highly penn'd": lyrics written in a courtly cavalier style or by courtiers of high birth, or both.

210. "lute": stringed musical instrument much used in Elizabethan times; it has a long neck and a hollow resonant body, and is played with the fingers of one hand or with a plectrum.

229. Hotspur imitates Mortimer's method of laying, or lying, only to make fun of him and his passionate and demonstrative Welsh wife: he and Kate are much less demonstrative, as is shown by her calling him a giddy goose. The differences between the Welsh and the English temperaments is here shown.

233. "humorous": moody.

236. "humours": moods.

248. "comfit-maker's": sweetmeat or confectionery-maker's.

251. "sarcenet": fine soft silk material.

252. "Finsbury": district in London noted for its middle-class wealth and tradespeople. As a great landowner and a brave countryman, Hotspur scorned city life and culture.

HENRY IV, 1

ACT III SCENE I

ACT III SCENE II

Back at the royal palace in London, King Henry IV and the Prince of Wales have the interview which has been parodied by the Prince with Falstaff the night before.

As might be expected, the King begins to accuse the Prince, his son, of having been sent by God to punish him for his own misdeeds. How else could the Prince's activities be explained? Why else should he pursue such barren pleasures, and keep such low and disorderly company?

The language is dignified and the meter regular blank verse, to match the manner of the King who is being very majestic and forbidding. Hal listens patiently while his father rolls melodiously on.

Hal asks his father not to listen to false tales about his son's conduct, and to listen to Hal's own account of what he has been truly charged with. Hal does not deny that in his youth he has "faulty wander'd and irregular" and asks for pardon on his true submission.

He wonders why his son has been so unlike his ancestors in choosing common, low company, so that he has been replaced by his younger brother in the council of state, and is marked out as a probable failure when he succeeds to the throne. This deeply grieves his father, who goes on to draw a picture of himself when young. He was seldom seen in public, so that when he did make an appearance people gazed at him as if he were a comet to be wondered at.

Swear me, Kate, like a lady as thou art.
A good mouth-filling oath, and leave 'in sooth',
And such protest of pepper-gingerbread,
To velvet-guards and Sunday-citizens.   256
Come, sing.
Lady Percy. I will not sing.
Hotspur. 'Tis the next way to turn tailor, or be red-breast teacher. An the indentures be drawn, I'll away within these two hours; and so, come in when ye will.
                  [*Exit.*
Glendower. Come, come, Lord Mortimer; you are as slow
As hot Lord Percy is on fire to go.   263
By this our book is drawn; we'll but seal,
And then to horse immediately.
Mortimer.   With all my heart.   [*Exeunt.*

Scene two.

(LONDON. THE PALACE.)

Enter the KING, PRINCE OF WALES, *and* Others.

King. Lords, give us leave: the Prince of Wales and I
Must have some private conference; but be near at hand,
For we shall presently have need of you.
                [*Exeunt* Lords.
I know not whether God will have it so,
For some displeasing service I have done,
That, in his secret doom, out of my blood
He'll breed revengement and a scourge for me;
But thou dost in thy passages of life
Make me believe that thou art only mark'd
For the hot vengeance and the rod of heaven
To punish my mistreadings. Tell me else,
Could such inordinate and low desires,   12
Such poor, such bare, such lewd, such mean attempts,
Such barren pleasures, rude society,
As thou art match'd withal and grafted to,
Accompany the greatness of thy blood
And hold their level with thy princely heart?
Prince. So please your majesty, I would I could
Quit all offences with as clear excuse
As well as I am doubtless I can purge
Myself of many I am charged withal:
Yet such extenuation let me beg,   22
As, in reproof of many tales devised,
Which oft the ear of greatness needs must hear,
By smiling pick-thanks and base newsmongers,
I may, for some things true, wherein my youth
Hath faulty wander'd and irregular,
Find pardon on my true submission.
King. God pardon thee! yet let me wonder, Harry,
At thy affections, which do hold a wing
Quite from the flight of all thy ancestors.
Thy place in council thou hast rudely lost,
Which by thy younger brother is supplied,

256. "velvet-guards": wearers of velvet trimmings or such finery.

263. "hot Lord Percy": a punning reference to Hotspur.

12. "inordinate": out of the limits of order.

22. "extenuation": something that lessens the seriousness of the offense.

HENRY IV, 1

ACT III SCENE II

Men would not recognize him in public, for he appeared there so rarely and was so humble when he did so that they would all crane their necks to see this Bolingbroke. Even in the presence of the King, men gave him their allegiance because they liked and trusted him. They did not admire or trust Richard II as much as Bolingbroke, which is the main reason why they later invited Bolingbroke to become king instead of Richard's choice, Mortimer.

Richard was "the skipping king" who ambled up and down listening to shallow jesters and rash bavin wits; he went out so often, played the fool so rashly, and was so well-known that people began to grow tired of him and lost their respect for the throne. He was as commonly heard as is the English cuckoo in June, "heard, not regarded."

Shakespeare is always at home when writing of the duties of kingship, and in the comparisons he draws in this speech he reveals a deep reverence for and understanding of the monarchy. This would certainly have appealed to Queen Elizabeth I and her chief courtiers, as well as to her audience (except for those who harbored, even then, republican sympathies).

The crux of the King's argument comes in line 85, when he compares Prince Hal to the irresponsible Richard as he was then, for he has lost his princely privilege with participation in vile and ungentlemanly activities. Perhaps the King has the Gadshill episode in mind, for the report of this must have reached him in one form or another by now.

And art almost an alien to the hearts 34
Of all the court and princes of my blood:
The hope and expectation of thy time
Is ruin'd, and the soul of every man
Prophetically do forethink thy fall.
Had I so lavish of my presence been,
So common-hackney'd in the eyes of men,
So stale and cheap to vulgar company,
Opinion, that did help me to the crown,
Had still kept loyal to possession
And left me in reputeless banishment,
A fellow of no mark nor likelihood.
By being seldom seen, I could not stir
But like a comet I was wonder'd at; 47
That men would tell their children 'This is he';
Others would say 'Where, which is Bolingbroke?'
And then I stole all courtesy from heaven,
And dress'd myself in such humility
That I did pluck allegiance from men's hearts,
Loud shouts and salutations from their mouths,
Even in the presence of the crowned king.
Thus did I keep my person fresh and new;
My presence, like a robe pontifical, 56
Ne'er seen but wonder'd at: and so my state,
Seldom but sumptuous, showed like a feast 58
And won by rareness such solemnity.
The skipping king, he ambled up and down 60
With shallow jesters and rash bavin wits, 61
Soon kindled and soon burnt; carded his state, 62
Mingled his royalty with capering fools,
Had his great name profaned with their scorns
And gave his countenance, against his name,
To laugh at gibing boys and stand the push
Of every beardless vain comparative,
Grew a companion to the common streets,
Enfeoff'd himself to popularity; 69
That, being daily swallow'd by men's eyes,
They surfeited with honey and began
To loathe the taste of sweetness, whereof a little
More than a little is by much too much.
So when he had occasion to be seen,
He was but as the cuckoo is in June, 75
Heard, not regarded; seen, but with such eyes
As, sick and blunted with community,
Afford no extraordinary gaze,
Such as is bent on sun-like majesty
When it shines seldom in admiring eyes;
But rather drowsed and hung their eyelids down,
Slept in his face and render'd such aspect
As cloudy men use to their adversaries,
Being with his presence glutted, gorged and full.
And in that very line, Harry, standest thou; 85
For thou hast lost thy princely privilege
With vile participation: not an eye
But is a-weary of thy common sight,
Save mine, which hath desired to see thee more;
Which now doth that I would not have it do,
Make blind itself with foolish tenderness.
   Prince. I shall hereafter, my thrice gracious lord,
Be more myself.

34. "alien": foreigner.

47. "comet": shooting star trailing a tail of light.

56. "pontifical": pertaining to a bishop or a pope.

58. Seldom but Sumptuous, Showed like a feaSt And won by rareneSS Such Solemnity, NOTE the alliteration of the sibilant—S sound, to achieve the desired effect of solemnity. (See contrast with l. 60).

60. "skipping king": gives an effect of light-heartedness and irresponsibility.

61. "bavin": brushwood, faggots ('soon ablaze').

62. "carded": mixed with something base. The word was in use from 1590 to 1635 for mixing different kinds of drink.

69. "Enfeoff'd himself": surrendered himself.

75. "cuckoo": bird common in June hence ignored.

HENRY IV, 1

ACT III SCENE II

If Hal resembles the vanquished Richard, Hotspur looks like Bolingbroke as he was when he landed at Ravenspurgh. The irony of this situation, expressed by Hal's lack of interest in the inheritance as compared with Hotspur's passionate interest in it, is bitter to the King, who sees the historical parallels very clearly, Shakespeare exaggerates these historical parallels for the sake of their dramatic effect.

Henry continues to praise Hotspur's valor, especially for the honor he won by fighting the renowned Earl of Douglas. It is plain that he feels his own son Hal is vastly inferior to Hotspur of the north.

Henry goes on to describe how Hotspur, "this Mars in swathling clothes," and Douglas have struck up an alliance, to which many others belong, including Percy, Northumberland, the Archbishop of York, Mortimer and others, to oppose the royal forces in civil war. He stops and asks why he should reveal this news to his son, who is his "nearest and dearest enemy." He says he knows that his son will probably join the Percies against his own father, to show how much he has fallen away from his standards.

The accusation of disloyalty, and the unfavorable comparison just made between himself and Hotspur, are too much for Hal, and he comes forward with an intense speech against those who have turned the King away from his own son. He promises to redeem all this on Percy's head, and in the closing of some glorious day he will be bold enough to tell his father that he is a true son.

The King is overjoyed at this attitude of his son's, but does not yet know whether to believe it.

Hal goes on to declare that the time will come when he will make this northern youth (Hotspur) exchange his glorious deeds for Hal's indignities. He makes a sol-

---

King.   For all the world
As thou art to this hour was Richard then
When I from France set foot at Ravenspurgh,   95
And even as I was then is Percy now.
Now, by my sceptre and my soul to boot,
He hath more worthy interest to the state
Than thou the shadow of succession:
For of no right, nor colour like to right,
He doth fill fields with harness in the realm,
Turns head against the lion's armed jaws,
And, being no more in debt to years than thou,
Leads ancient lords and reverend bishops on
To bloody battles and to bruising arms.
What never-dying honour hath he got
Against renowned Douglas! whose high deeds,
Whose hot incursions and great name in arms   108
Holds from all soldiers chief majority
And military title capital
Through all the kingdoms that acknowledge Christ:
Thrice hath this Hotspur, Mars in swathling clothes, 112
This infant warrior, in his enterprises
Discomfited great Douglas, ta'en him once,
Enlarged him and made a friend of him,
To fill the mouth of deep defiance up
And shake the peace and safety of our throne.
And what say you to this? Percy, Northumberland,
The Archbishop's grace of York, Douglas, Mortimer,
Capitulate against us and are up.   120
But wherefore do I tell these news to thee?
Why, Harry, do I tell thee of my foes,
Which art my near'st and dearest enemy?
Thou that art like enough, through vassal fear,
Base inclination and the start of spleen,
To fight against me under Percy's pay,
To dog his heels and curtsy at his frowns,
To show how much thou art degenerate.

Prince. Do not think so; you shall not find it so:
And God forgive them that so much have sway'd
Your majesty's good thoughts away from me!
I will redeem all this on Percy's head
And in the closing of some glorious day
Be bold to tell you that I am your son;
When I will wear a garment all of blood
And stain my favours in a bloody mask,
Which, wash'd away, shall scour my shame with it:
And that shall be the day, whene'er it lights,
That this same child of honour and renown,
This gallant Hotspur, this all-praised knight,
And your unthought-of Harry chance to meet.
For every honour sitting on his helm,   142
Would they were multitudes, and on my head
My shames redoubled! for the time will come,
That I shall make this northern youth exchange
His glorious deeds for my indignities.
Percy is but my factor, good my lord,   147
To engross up glorious deeds on my behalf;
And I will call him to so strict account,   149
That he shall render every glory up,
Yea, even the slightese worship of his time,
Or I will tear the reckoning from his heart.   152

---

95. "Ravenspurgh": a port which has long since disappeared owing to silting up; its site is now several miles inland.

108. "incursions": runnings-in.

112. "Mars": Greek god of war. "swathling clothes": wrappings of an infant.

120. "Capitulate": literally head together. "up": up in arms.

142. "helm": helmet.

147. "factor": person who does business for another at buying or selling on commission (hence the reference in line 149 to 'so strict account') followed by line 152 'reckoning'.

HENRY IV, 1

ACT III SCENE II

emn oath to call Percy to a strict account, and his father is delighted.

The King decides to give his son full authority to do what he promises, and hopes it will lead to the deaths of a hundred thousand rebels.

Sir Walter Blunt enters hurriedly, and reports that Lord Mortimer of Scotland has sent word that the Earl of Douglas and the English rebels met on the eleventh day of the month at Shrewsbury, and constitute a single force that is mighty and fearful.

Henry sends the Earl of Westmoreland and Prince John of Lancaster to advance north with an army to Shrewsbury. Harry (which is the name Henry uses for his son) is to advance on Wednesday next; the day following the King himself will set out and Bridgenorth will be the meeting place. Harry shall march through Gloucestershire and in twelve days they shall meet. Henry's urgent speech, full of decision and command, ends on a brisk rhymed couplet.

ACT III SCENE III

At the Boar's Head Tavern in Eastcheap Falstaff is in a fretful state, and is complaining to Bardolph. He says he is growing thin, and threatens to repent of his sins and turn religious. This is a side of Falstaff that we have never seen before, and do not easily associate with his character as a bon-vivant. He blames it on the villainous company he has been keeping lately, but Bardolph ascribes his melancholy to his fatness.

This, in the name of God, I promise here:
The which if He be pleased I shall perform,
I do beseech your majesty may salve   155
The long-grown wounds of my intemperance:
If not, the end of life cancels all bands;
And I will die a hundred thousand deaths
Ere break the smallest parcel of this vow.

King. A hundred thousand rebels die in this:
Thou shalt have charge and sovereign trust herein.

Enter BLUNT.

How now, good Blunt? thy looks are full of speed.

Blunt. So hath the business that I come to speak of.
Lord Mortimer of Scotland hath sent word
That Douglas and the English rebels met
The eleventh of this month at Shrewsbury:
A mighty and fearful head they are,   167
If promises be kept on every hand,
As ever offer'd foul play in a state.

King. The Earl of Westmoreland set forth to-day;
With him my son, Lord John of Lancaster;
For this advertisement is five days old: 172
On Wednesday next, Harry, you shall set forward;
On Thursday we ourselves will march: our meeting
In Bridgenorth: and, Harry, you shall march
Through Gloucestershire; by which account,
Our business valued, some twelve days hence
Our general forces at Bridgenorth shall meet.
Our hands are full of business: let's away:
Advantage feeds him fat while men delay.   [*Exeunt.*

Scene three.

(EASTCHEAP. THE BOAR'S-HEAD TAVERN.)

Enter FALSTAFF *and* BARDOLPH.

Falstaff. Bardolph, am I not fallen away vilely since this last action? do I not bate? do I not dwindle?   2
Why, my skin hangs about me like an old lady's loose gown; I am withered like an old apple-john. Well, I'll repent, and that suddenly, while I am in some liking; I shall be out of heart shortly, and then I shall have no strength to repent. An I have not forgotten what the inside of a church is made of, I am a peppercorn, a brewer's horse; the inside of a church! Company, villainous company, hath been the spoil of me.

Bardolph. Sir John, you are so fretful, you cannot live long.

Falstaff. Why, there is it; come sing me a song; make me merry. I was as virtuously given as a gentleman need to be; virtuous enough; swore little; diced not above seven times a week; paid money that I borrowed, three or four times; lived well and in good compass; and now I live out of all order, out of all compass.

Bardolph. Why, you are so fat, Sir John, that you must needs be out of all compass, out of all reasonable compass, Sir John.

Falstaff. Do thou amend thy face, and I'll amend

---

155. "salve": heal (with soothing ointment).

167. "head": military force.

172. "advertisement": news or information.

2. "bate": decrease, fall off, abate.

HENRY IV, 1

ACT III SCENE III

It does not take Falstaff long, however, to start insulting Bardolph's red face which resembles the lantern in the poop of the admiral's flagship at night, and makes him seem the Knight of the Burning Lamp. There follows a hilarious speech about the redness of Bardolph's face, which has saved Falstaff money otherwise spent on links and torches, but has cost him more than he saved on the liquor with which he has kept Bardolph supplied (so he claims) for these last thirty-two years.

Mistress Quickly, called Dame Partlet, enters, and Falstaff asks her if she found out who picked his pocket. She says she does not keep thieves in her public house, and has made all sorts of inquiries but has not discovered who did it.

It becomes evident that Falstaff is picking a quarrel with the Hostess to distract her attention away from the fact that he owes her money, and cannot pay it now. She sees through him, however, and claims her bill and the cost of a dozen shirts she bought him. He claims that they were of inferior quality, but this is quite an irrelevant consideration. Falstaff owes £24/0/0, a large sum for those days merely for eating and drinking, though it included a personal loan.

Falstaff tells Bardolph to pay this bill, but Mistress Quickly says that Bardolph is only a poor man. Then Falstaff begins to quibble about a seal-ring he lost at the inn, that was worth forty marks. The Hostess says she has often heard the Prince tell Falstaff this ring was made of copper, not gold, and Falstaff curses the Prince.

---

my life: thou art our admiral, thou bearest the lantern in the poop, but 'tis in the nose of thee; thou art the Knight of the Burning Lamp.

Bardolph. Why, Sir John, my face does you no harm.

Falstaff. No, I'll be sworn; I make as good use of it as many a man doth of a Death's-head or a memento mori: I never see thy face but I think upon hell-fire and Dives that lived in purple; for there he is in his robes, burning, burning. If thou wert any way given to virtue, I would swear by thy face; my oath should be 'By this fire, that's God's angel': but thou art altogether given over, and wert indeed, but for the light in thy face, the son of utter darkness. When thou rannest up Gadshill in the night to catch my horse, if I did not think thou hadst been an ignis fatuus or a ball of wildfire, there's no purchase in money. O, thou art a perpetual triumph, an everlasting bonfirelight! Thou hast saved me a thousand marks in links and torches, walking with thee in the night betwixt tavern and tavern: but the sack that thou hast drunk me would have bought me lights as good cheap at the dearest chandler's in Europe. I have maintained that salamander of yours with fire any time this two and thirty years; God reward me for it!

Bardolph. 'Sblood, I would my face were in your stomach!

Falstaff. God-a-mercy! so should I be sure to be heartburned.

Enter Hostess.

How now, Dame Partlet the hen! have you inquired yet who picked my pocket?

Hostess. Why, Sir John, what do you think, Sir John? do you think I keep thieves in my house? I have searched, I have inquired, so has my husband, man by man, boy by boy, servant by servant: the tithe of a hair was never lost in my house before.

Falstaff. Ye lie, hostess: Bardolph was shaved and lost many a hair; and I'll be sworn my pocket was picked. Go to, you are a woman, go.

Hostess. Who, I? no; I defy thee: God's light, I was never called so in mine own house before.

Falstaff. Go to, I know you well enough.

Hostess. No, Sir John: you do not know me, Sir John. I know you, Sir John; you owe me money, Sir John; and now you pick a quarrel to beguile me of it: I bought you a dozen shirts to your back.

Falstaff. Dowlas, filthy dowlas: I have given them away to bakers' wives, and they have made bolters of them.

Hostess. Now, as I am a true woman, holland of eight shillings an ell. You owe money here besides, Sir John, for your diet and by-drinkings, and money lent you, four and twenty pound.

Falstaff. He had his part of it; let him pay.

Hostess. He? alas, he is poor; he hath nothing.

Falstaff. How! poor? look upon his face; what call you rich? let them coin his nose, let them coin his cheeks: I'll not pay a denier. What, will you make a younker of me? shall I not take mine ease in mine inn but I shall have my pocket picked? I have lost a

---

29

30

31

38

45

46

52

69

70

72

73

80

81

29-30. "memento mori": reminder of death (usually a skull).

31. "Dives": the wealthy man in the parable of Dives and Lazarus.

38. "ignis fatuus": fools' fire or will o' the wisp, caused by burning marsh-gas.

45. "chandler's": candlestick-maker's.

46. "salamander": person who likes or can stand a great deal of heat, or spirit or other imaginary being that lives in fire (used humorously).

52. "Dame Partlet": Chaucerian reference from the French.

69. "dowlas": coarse linen.

70. "bolters": sieves for sifting flour from bran.

72. "holland": fine linen.

73. "ell": 45 inches.

80. "denier": smallest English coin.

81. "younker": sucker (colloquial).

HENRY IV, 1

ACT III SCENE III

At this very moment in march the Prince and Peto, as if on parade, and Falstaff meets them playing on his truncheon like a military fife.

Falstaff addresses the Prince before Mistress Quickly can voice her complaint. He tells of having his pocket picked, but the Prince dismisses it as a trivial matter. The Hostess bursts out that Falstaff has been talking most foully about the Prince, and has threatened to cudgel him. Falstaff denies everything and accuses the inn-keeper's wife of making this up. He sends her away with some bawdy humor.

The Prince of Wales takes the Hostess' side in this dispute against Falstaff. Bardolph sides against him too, and the Prince calls his bluff. They jest on about Falstaff's disgraceful but highly characteristic accusation, until Falstaff finds enough confidence to send the woman away, and she goes willingly.

sealring of my grandfather's worth forty mark.

Hostess. O Jesu, I have heard the prince tell him, I know not how oft, that that ring was copper!

Falstaff. How! the prince is a Jack, a neak-cup: 'sblood, an he were here, I would cudgel him like a dog, if he would say so.

Enter the PRINCE *and* PETO, *marching, and* FALSTAFF *meets them playing on his truncheon like a fife.*

How now, lad! is the wind in that door, i' faith? must we all march?

Bardolph. Yea, two and two, Newgate fashion. 91

Hostess. My lord, I pray you, hear me.

Prince. What sayst thou, Mistress Quickly? How doth thy husband? I love him well; he is an honest man.

Hostess. Good my lord, hear me.

Falstaff. Prithee, let her alone, and list to me.

Prince. What sayest thou Jack?

Falstaff. The other night I fell asleep here behind the arras and had my pocket picked. 100

Prince. What didst thou lose, Jack?

Falstaff. Wilt thou believe me, Hal? three or four bonds of forty pound a-piece, and a seal-ring of my grandfather's.

Prince. A trifle, some eight-penny matter.

Hostess. So I told him, my lord; and I said I heard your grace say so: and, my lord, he speaks most vilely of you, like a foul-mouthed man as he is; and said that he would cudgel you.

Prince. What! he did not?

Hostess. There's neither faith, truth, nor womanhood in me else.

Falstaff. There's no more faith in thee than in a stewed prune; nor no more truth in thee than in a drawn fox; and for womanhood, Maid Marian may 115 be the deputy's wife of the ward to thee. Go, you thing, go.

Hostess. Say, what thing? what thing?

Falstaff. What thing! why, a thing to thank God on.

Hostess. I am no thing to thank God on, I would thou shouldst know it; I am an honest man's wife: and setting thy knighthood aside, thou art a knave to call me so.

Prince. Thou sayest true, hostess; and he slanders 124 thee most grossly.

Hostess. So he doth you, my lord; and said this other day you ought him a thousand pound.

Prince. Sirrah, do I owe you a thousand pound?

Falstaff. A thousand pound, Hal! a million: thy love is worth a million: thou owest me thy love.

Hostess. Nay, my lord, he called you Jack, and said he would cudgel you.

Falstaff. Did I, Bardolph?

Bardolph. Indeed, Sir John, you said so.

Falstaff. Yea, if he said my ring was copper.

Prince. I say 'tis copper: darest thou be as good as thy word now?

Falstaff. Why, Hal, thou know'st, as thou art but man, I dare; but as thou art prince, I fear thee as I fear the roaring of the lion's whelp.

86. "neak-cup": sneak-cup, one who steals cups from taverns.

91. "Newgate": old London prison.

100. "arras": wall-hanging tapestry.

115. "Maid Marian": the woman in Robin Hood's gang, usually played by a lumpish man in the morris dance referred to here.

124. "slanders": spreads a false statement calculated to do harm.

HENRY IV, 1

ACT III SCENE III

Falstaff questions Hal about the robbery, and the Prince assures him that all the money has been repaid. Hal is now good friends with the King and may do anything. He tells Falstaff he has procured him the charge of foot he mentioned earlier, and Falstaff says he wishes it could have been of horse.

If Falstaff is an infantry captain now, Bardolph becomes the bearer of important dispatches. He has to take them to Prince John and to the Earl of Westmoreland. Peto and the Prince have to ride thirty miles before dinner, but before leaving the Prince makes an appointment to meet Falstaff in the temple hall at two o'clock tomorrow afternoon. He will receive his commission, his men, and money and order for their equipment. The country is on fire; Percy stands on high; either the rebels or the king's men must lower lie.

Listening to this dynamic and animated speech, Falstaff makes a cynical comment:

Rare words! brave world! Hostess, my breakfast, come!

O, I could wish this tavern were my drum!

This reflection on honor is an important one when we come to consider the theme of this play, which involves various opposing views of the nature of chivalry and honor.

Prince. And why not as the lion?

Falstaff. The king himself is to be feared as the lion: dost thou think I'll fear thee as I fear thy father? nay, an I do, I pray God my girdle break.

Prince. O, if it should! But, sirrah, there's no room for faith, truth, nor honesty in this bosom of thine. Charge an honest woman with picking thy pocket! why, thou impudent, embossed rascal, if there were 148 anything in thy pocket but tavern-reckonings, and one poor pennyworth of sugar-candy to make thee long-winded, if thy pocket were enriched with any other injuries but these, I am a villain: and yet you will stand to it; you will not pocket up wrong: art thou not ashamed?

Falstaff. Dost thou hear, Hal? thou knowest in the state of innocency Adam fell; and what should poor Jack Falstaff do in the days of villainy? Thou seest I have more flesh than another man, and therefore more frailty. You confess then, you picked my pocket?

Prince. It appears so by the story.

Falstaff. Hostess, I forgive thee; go, make ready breakfast, love thy husband, look to thy servants, cherish thy guests: thou shalt find me tractable to any honest reason: thou seest I am pacified still. Nay, prithee, begone. [*Exit* Hostess.] Now, Hal, to the news at court: for the robbery, lad, how is that answered?

Prince. O, my sweet beef, I must still be good angel to thee: the money is paid back again.

Falstaff. O, I do not like that paying back; 'tis a double labour.

Prince. I am good friends with my father and may do any thing.

Falstaff. Rob me the exchequer the first thing thou doest, and do it with unwashed hands too.

Bardolph. Do, my lord.

Prince. I have procured thee, Jack, a charge of foot. 177

Falstaff. I would it had been of horse. Where shall I find one that can steal well? O for a fine thief, of the age of two and twenty or thereabouts! I am heinously unprovided. Well, God be thanked for these rebels, they offend none but the virtuous: I laud them, I praise them.

Prince. Bardolph!

Bardolph. My lord?

Prince. Go bear this letter to Lord John of Lancaster, to my brother John; this to my Lord of Westmoreland. [*Exit* BARDOLPH.] Go, Peto, to horse, to horse; for thou and I have thirty miles to ride yet ere dinner time. [*Exit* PETO.] Jack, meet me tomorrow in the temple hall at two o'clock in the 191 afternoon.

There shalt thou know thy charge; and there receive Money and order for their furniture.

The land is burning; Percy stands on high;

And either we or they must lower lie.   [*Exit.*

Falstaff. Rare words! brave world! Hostess, my breakfast, come!

O, I could wish this tavern were my drum!   [*Exit.*

148. "embossed": rounded and pressed out (a reference to Falstaff's fatness).

177. "charge of foot": a company of infantrymen.

191. "temple hall": Temple Hall, headquarters of the ancient order of Knights Templar of St. John of Jerusalem.

HENRY IV, 1

ACT IV SCENE I

The rebels are encamped at Shrewsbury, a convenient meeting place for those who come from north, central and southern England, and Wales.

Hotspur is praising the Earl of Douglas to his face, and the brave earl replies calling Hotspur "the king of honour."

Hotspur and Douglas are two of a kind, brave, bold, impetuous men of action and in love with honor, but lacking the capacity to plan ahead; essentially idealistic, they lack common sense.

A messenger enters bearing letters from Northumberland. The earl (Hotspur's father) is sick, and cannot make the journey to Shrewsbury as arranged. Hotspur has no patience with illness, and voices his disappointment loudly instead of reading the letters.

Worcester realizes the seriousness of Northumberland's illness for the rebel cause. Hotspur says "this sickness now doth infect/The very lifeblood of our enterprise." The old sick man (probably dying) nevertheless urges Hotspur and the others to go on with the rebellion, to find out what fate has in store for them, because they cannot give up now since the king has almost certainly heard about their intentions.

This is the first blow struck at the rebel cause, and a very grave one. But others follow soon.

ACT FOUR, scene one.

(THE REBEL CAMP NEAR SHREWSBURY.)

Enter HOTSPUR, WORCESTER, *and* DOUGLAS.

Hotspur. Well said, my noble Scot: if speaking truth
In this fine age were not thought flattery,
Such attribution should the Douglas have,
As not a soldier of this season's stamp
Should go so general current through the world.
By God, I cannot flatter; I do defy
The tongues of soothers; but a braver place
In my heart's love hath no man than yourself:
Nay, task me to my word; approve me, lord.
Douglas. Thou art the king of honour:
No man so potent breathes upon the ground
But I will beard him.
Hotspur.   Do so, and 'tis well.

Enter a Messenger *with letters.*

What letters hast thou there?—I can but thank you.
Messenger. These letters come from your father.   14
Hotspur. Letters from him! why comes he not
    himself?
Messenger. He cannot come, my lord; he is grievous
    sick.
Hotspur. 'Zounds! how has he the leisure to be sick?   17
In such a justling time? Who leads his power?
Under whose government come they along?
Messenger. His letters bear his mind, not I, my
    lord.
Worcester. I prithee, tell me, doth he keep his bed?
Messenger. He did, my lord, four days ere I set
    forth;
And at the time of my departure thence
He was much fear'd by his physicians.   24
Worcester. I would the state of time had first been   25
    whole
Ere he by sickness had been visited:
His health was never better worth than now.
Hotspur. Sick now! droop now! this sickness doth
    infect
The very life-blood of our enterprise;
'Tis catching hither, even to our camp.
He writes me here, that inward sickness—
And that his friends by deputation could not
So soon be drawn, nor did he think it meet
To lay so dangerous and dear a trust
On any soul removed but on his own
Yet doth he give us bold advertisement,   36
That with our small conjunction we should on,
To see how fortune is disposed to us;
For, as he writes, there is no quailing now,   39
Because the king is certainly possess'd   40
Of all our purposes. What say you to it?
Worcester. Your father's sickness is a maim to us.   42
Hotspur. A perilous gash, a very limb lopp'd off
And yet, in faith, it is not; his present want

---

14. "father": the Earl of Northumberland.

17. "leisure to be sick": Hotspur assumes his father is malingering.

24. "He was": his life was feared (of).

25. "whole": the rebellion had been wholly completed.

36. "advertisement": advice, counsel (stress falls on the second syllable).

39. "quailing": cowardly giving up.

40. "possess'd": in full possession of.

42. "maim": crippling disfiguring wound (sustained in line 43, 'a perilous gash, a very limp lopp'd off').

63

HENRY IV, 1

ACT IV SCENE I

Hotspur sees some good in the non-arrival of the Earl of Northumberland and his force; at least, if the rebel army is defeated at Shrewsbury, they will have a substantial force to fall back on as reinforcement, and will not have put all their eggs in the same basket, so to speak. He calls the Northumberland force a "sweet reversion." "A comfort of retirement lies in this."

Worcester sees, however, that the rebel force is so small that it cannot afford to be divided at this point. He knows that the common people will suspect Northumberland of fearing the outcome of the rebellion and, therefore, of absenting himself using illness as his excuse. It may breed a kind of question in the cause, or even show a kind of fear not before dreamt of.

Hotspur is more optimistic than Worcester about the turn affairs have taken. Northumberland's absence lends a luster and a larger dare to this great enterprise. Douglas agrees with him; the word fear does not figure in the Scottish vocabulary.

Sir Richard Vernon enters with more news: the Earl of Westmoreland and Prince John of Lancaster are marching towards the rebel force with an army seven thousand strong. The king himself will soon be traveling northwards also. The nimble-footed, madcap Prince of Wales is also armed, and on the way. The king's men are "all plumed like" ostriches, and glitter in their golden coats, like icons.

Seems more than we shall find it: were it good
To set the exact wealth of all our states
All at one cast? to set so rich a main   47
On the nice hazard of one doubtful hour?   48
It were not good; for therein should we read
The very bottom and the soul of hope,
The very list, the very utmost bound
Of all our fortunes.
  Douglas.   'Faith, and so we should;
Where now remains a sweet reversion:
We may boldly spend upon the hope of what
Is to come in:
A comfort of retirement lives in this.
  Hotspur. A rendezvous, a home to fly unto,   57
If that the devil and mischance look big
Upon our affairs.
  Worcester. But yet I would your father had been
       here.
The quality and hair of our attempt
Brooks no division: it will be thought
By some that know not why he is away,
That wisdom, loyalty and mere dislike
Of our proceedings kept the earl from hence
And think how such an apprehension
May turn the tide of fearless faction
And breed a kind of question in our cause;
For well you know we of the offering side
Must keep aloof from strict arbitrement,   70
And stop all sight-holes, every loop from whence
The eye of reason may pry in upon us:
This absence of your father's draws a curtain,
That shows the ignorant a kind of fear
Before not dreamt of.
  Hotspur.   You strain too far.
I rather of his absence make this use:
It lends a lustre and more great opinion,
A larger dare to our great enterprise,   78
Than if the earl were here; for men must think,
If we without his help can make a head   80
To push against a kingdom, with his help
We shall o'erturn it topsy-turvy down.
Yet all goes well, yet all our joints are whole.
  Douglas. As heart can think: there is not such a word
Spoke of in Scotland as this term of fear.

         Enter SIR RICHARD VERNON.

Hotspur. My cousin Vernon! welcome, by my soul.
Vernon. Pray God my news be worth a welcome,
     lord.
The Earl of Westmoreland, seven thousand strong,
Is marching hitherwards; with him Prince John.
Hotspur. No harm: what more?
Vernon.   And further, I have learn'd
The king himself in person is set forth,
Or hitherwards intended speedily,
With strong and mighty preparation.
Hotspur. He shall be welcome too. Where is his son,
The nimble-footed, madcap Prince of Wales,   95
And his comrades, that daff'd the world aside,
And bid it pass?
  Vernon.   All furnish'd, all in arms;

47. "main": prize or reward.

48. "nice hazard": delicate risk. "one doubtful hour": the actual battle.

57. "rendezvous": meeting place.

70. "arbitrement": judgment.

78. "larger dare": bigger challenge.

80. "make a head": raise an army.

95. "nimble-footed": madcap, the unreformed Prince (news of his reformation has not yet penetrated northwards).

64

HENRY IV, 1

ACT IV SCENE I

The royal army is as full of spirit as the month of May; there follows a heroic account of young Harry with full armor on "rise from the ground like feather'd Mercury" and vault with such ease into his seat on the charger that it seemed as if an angel dropped down from the clouds,

"To turn and wind a fiery Pegasus and witch the world with noble horsemanship." Hotspur cannot bear this poetic description of his arch-enemy, which comes to him "worse than the sun in March." He says let them come as to a sacrifice; he will fight the Prince of Wales in mortal combat; "Harry to Harry shall, hot horse to horse,/Meet and ne'er part till one drop down a corse."

More news arrives; Glendower will take a further fourteen days to marshal his force. This is really the worst news of all, since the battle cannot be deferred so long.

Vernon estimates that the royal army numbers thirty thousand armed men. Be it forty thousand, Hotspur is ready for them. But his readiness is merely emotional, not strategic. He calls for a muster-parade to see how many men he has in fighting condition, and says "Doomsday is near; die all, die merrily."

Douglas says talk not of dying; for the next six months he has forgotten the fear of dying.

ACT IV SCENE II

Shakespeare takes us over to a point on the road between London and Shrewsbury, not far from Coventry in Warwickshire.

Dressed in infantry uniforms, Falstaff as a captain and Bardolph as a corporal make plans for solving their drinking problem. Bardolph is being sent on ahead to purchase a bottle of sack, and asks Falstaff for the money; it will cost at least an angel. The men

---

All plumed like estridges that wing the wind,   98
Bated like eagles having lately bathed;
Glittering in golden coats, like images;
As full of spirit as the month of May,
And gorgeous as the sun at midsummer;
Sportive as youthful goats, wild as young bulls.
I saw young Harry, with his beaver on,   104
His cuisses on his thighs, gallantly arm'd,   105
Rise from the ground like feather'd Mercury,   106
And vaulted with such ease into his seat,   107
As if an angel dropp'd down from the clouds,
To turn and wind a fiery Pegasus   109
And witch the world with noble horsemanship.   110
   Hotspur. No more, no more: worse than the sun in
      March,
This praise doth nourish agues. Let them come;
They come like sacrifices in their trim,
And to the fire-eyed maid of smoky war
All hot and bleeding will we offer them:
The mailed Mars shall on his altar sit
Up to the ears in blood. I am on fire
To hear this rich reprisal is so nigh   118
And yet not ours. Come, let me taste my horse,
Who is to bear me like a thunderbolt
Against the bosom of the Prince of Wales:
Harry to Harry shall, hot horse to horse,
Meet and ne'er part till one drop down a corse.
O that Glendower were come!
   Vernon.   There is more news:
I learn'd in Worcester, as I rode along,
He cannot draw his power this fourteen days.   126
   Douglas. That's the worse tidings that I hear of yet.
   Worcester. Ay, by my faith, that bears a frosty sound.
   Hotspur. What may the king's whole battle reach
      unto?
   Vernon. To thirty thousand.
   Hotspur.   Forty let it be:
My father and Glendower being both away,
The power of us may serve so great a day.
Come, let us take a muster speedily: 133
Doomsday is near; die all, die merrily.
   Douglas. Talk not of dying: I am out of fear
Of death or death's hand for this one half-year.
                        [*Exeunt.*

Scene two.

(A PUBLIC ROAD NEAR COVENTRY.)

Enter FALSTAFF *and* BARDOLPH.

Falstaff. Bardolph, get thee before to Coventry; fill me a bottle of sack: our soldiers shall march through; we'll to Sutton Co'fil' tonight.   3
   Bardolph. Will you give me money, captain?
   Falstaff. Lay out, lay out.
   Bardolph. This bottle makes an angel.   6
   Falstaff. An if it do, take if for thy labour; and if it make twenty, take them all, I'll answer the coinage.

---

98. "estridges": ostriches.

104. "beaver": face-guard of a helmet.

105. "cuisses": thigh-shields or plates.

106. "Mercury": messenger of the gods (feathered for fast arrow-like flight).

107. "vaulted": using a pole to get onto his saddle rather that being hoisted on a chain and pulley arrangement.

109. "Pegasus": the winged horse of poetry.

110. "witch": bewitch or enchant.

118. "rich reprisal": rich prize (to be taken).

126. "draw his power": muster his soldiers.

133. "muster": roll-call parade.

3. "Sutton Co'fil'": Sutton Coldfield north of Conventry in Warwickshire.

6. "angel": gold coin.

HENRY IV, 1

ACT IV SCENE II

are to march through Coventry and reach Sutton Coldfield by nightfall. Lieutenant Peto is to meet Falstaff at the town's end.

Falstaff is ashamed to take his soldiers through the town. He has been misusing the king's press, the method of conscripting able-bodied men into military service. He has permitted his original soldiers to purchase their freedom for £300 and odd pounds. He only conscripts men who have a good motive for not wanting to go away to the wars and who can afford to buy themselves out.

By this method Falstaff has exchanged one hundred and fifty good householders and yoemen's sons for a group of ancients, discarded unjust serving men, and a herd of tattered prodigals who look like scarecrows or hanged men torn down from the gallows. Falstaff refuses to march through Coventry with such a lot.

The Prince and the Earl of Westmoreland enter and find Falstaff there; he is taken by surprise, having thought that Prince Hal had already gone on to Shrewsbury.

Westmoreland is the commander-in-chief of the king's army, and he makes it clear that they should march all night to arrive at Shrewsbury as soon as possible. Hal asks who all these pitiful fellows are that follow after, and Falstaff claims them. Westmoreland says they are exceeding poor and bare, too beggarly for the wars.

Bid my lieutenant Peto meet me at town's end.

Bardolph. I will, captain: farewell.   *[Exit.*

Falstaff. If I be not ashamed of my soldiers, I am a soused gurnet. I have misused the king's press damnably. I have got, in exchange of a hundred and fifty soldiers, three hundred and odd pounds. I press me none but good householders, yeomen's sons; inquire me out contracted bachelors, such as had been asked twice on the banns; such a commodity of warm slaves, as had as lieve hear the devil as a drum; such as fear the report of a caliver worse that a struck fowl or a hurt wild-duck. I pressed me none but such toasts-and-butter, with hearts in their bodies no bigger than pins' heads, and they have bought out their services; and now my whole charge consists of ancients, corporals, lieutenants, gentlemen of companies, slaves as ragged as Lazarus in the painted cloth, where the glutton's dogs licked his sores; and such as indeed were never soldiers, but discarded unjust serving-men, younger sons to younger brothers, revolted tapsters and ostlers trade-fallen, the cankers of a calm world and a long peace, ten times more dishonourable ragged than an old faced ancient: and such have I, to fill up the rooms of them that have bought out their services, that you would think that I had a hundred and fifty tattered prodigals lately come from swine-keeping, from eating draff and husks. A mad fellow met me on the way and told me I had unloaded all the gibbets and pressed the dead bodies. No eye hath seen such scarecrows. I'll not march through Coventry with them, that's flat: nay, and the villains march wide betwixt the legs, as if they had gyves on; for indeed I had the most of them out of prison. There's but a shirt and a half in all my company; and the half shirt is two napkins tacked together and thrown over the shoulders like an herald's coat without sleeves; and the shirt, to say the truth, stolen from·my host at St. Alban's, or the red-nose innkeeper of Daventry. But that's all one; they'll find linen enough on every hedge.

Enter the PRINCE *and* WESTMORELAND.

Prince. How now, blown Jack! how now, quilt!

Falstaff. What, Hal! how now, mad wag! what a devil dost thou in Warwickshire? My good Lord of Westmoreland, I cry you mercy: I thought your honour had already been at Shrewsbury.

Westmoreland. Faith, Sir John, 'tis more than time that I were there, and you too; but my powers are there already. The king, I can tell you, looks for us all: we must away all night.

Falstaff. Tut, never fear me: I am as vigilant as a cat to steal cream.

Prince. I think, to steal cream indeed, for thy theft hath already made thee butter. But tell me, Jack, whose fellows are these that come after?

Falstaff. Mine, Hal, mine.

Prince. I did never see such pitiful rascals.

Falstaff. Tut, tut; good enough to toss; food for powder, food for powder; they'll fill a pit as well as better: tush man, mortal men, mortal men.

12

16

19
20

35

40

48

49

65
66

12. "soused gurnet": pickled fish (of little value).

16. "contracted bachelors": young men who are engaged to be married and whose banns are being called in church.

19. "caliver": light kind of musket or harquebus introduced during the sixteenth-century; it seems to have been the lightest portable fire-arm, except the pistol, and was fired without a 'rest' (Onions).

20-35. Falstaff refers to two parables, that of Dives and Lazarus, and that of the Prodigal Son.

40. "gyves": fetters, shackles.

48. "linen": shirts etc., placed on hedges to dry after having been washed.

49. "quilt": humorously applied to a fat person.

65-66. "food for powder": food for gunpowder.

HENRY IV, 1

ACT IV SCENE II

Falstaff says they are good enough for tossing into battle, as food for the gun powder or cannon fodder. Westmoreland and the Prince hurry off after this brief and light-hearted interchange, but Falstaff has the parting words: he looks forward to a speedy end to all fighting, and the beginning of the victory feast; this suits a dull fighter and a keen guest.

ACT IV SCENE III

At the rebel camp near Shrewsbury there is a dispute over whether to attack at once or to wait until morning. Hotspur wants to attack tonight, but Worcester thinks it would be more prudent to wait. Douglas not unnaturally supports Hotspur, but Vernon supports Worcester. Vernon is the only one able to describe the disadvantages of attacking forthwith; certain horse soldiers are expected to arrive soon, and the rebels need reinforcements; other horses that recently arrived need to be rested before going into battle. These practical considerations move Hotspur not at all; the king's horses are in the same state, he says.

Worcester's argument is convincing: the king's forces outnumber the rebel arms. They must wait for their other support to come in.

Westmoreland. Ay, but, Sir John, methinks they are exceeding poor and bare, too beggarly.

Falstaff. 'Faith, for their poverty, I know not where they had that; and for their bareness, I am sure they never learned that of me.

Prince. No, I'll be sworn; unless you call three fingers on the ribs bare. But, sirrah, make haste: Percy is already in the field.

Falstaff. What, is the king encamped?

Westmoreland. He is, Sir John: I fear we shall stay too long.

Falstaff. Well,
To the latter end of a fray and the beginning of a
    feast
Fits a dull fighter and keen guest.   [*Exeunt.*

Scene three.

(The Rebel Camp near Shrewsbury.)

Enter HOTSPUR, WORCESTER, DOUGLAS, *and* VERNON.

Hotspur. We'll fight with him to-night.
Worcester.   It may not be.
Douglas. You give him then advantage.
Vernon.   Not a whit.
Hotspur. Why say you so? looks he not for supply?   3
Vernon. So do we.
Hotspur.   His is certain, ours is doubtful.
Worcester. Good cousin, be advised; stir not to-night.
Vernon. Do not, my lord.
Douglas.   You do not counsel well:
You speak it out of fear and cold heart.
Vernon. Do me no slander, Douglas: by my life,
And I dare well maintain it with my life,
If well-respected honour bid me on,
I hold as little counsel with weak fear
As you, my lord, or any Scot that this day lives:
Let it be seen to-morrow in the battle
Which of us fears.
Douglas.   Yea, or to-night.
Vernon.   Content.
Hotspur. To-night, say I.
Vernon. Come, come, it may not be. I wonder much
Being men of such great leading as you are,
That you forsee not what impediments 18
Drag back our expedition: certain horse
Of my cousin Vernon's are not yet come up:
Your uncle Worcester's horse came but to-day;
And now their pride and mettle is asleep,
Their courage with hard labour tame and dull,
That not a horse is half the half of himself.
Hotspur. So are the horses of the enemy
In general, journey-bated and brought low: 26
The better part of ours are full of rest.
Worcester. The number of the king exceedeth ours:
For God's sake, cousin, stay till all come in.
            [*The trumpet sounds a parley.*

3. "supply": supplies of horses, equipment, food, and men.

18. "impediments": obstacles.

26. "journey-bated": tired out from traveling.

HENRY IV, 1

ACT IV SCENE III

The trumpet sounds a parley, and the king's messenger enters. He is old Sir Walter Blunt and he has come to try to persuade the rebel leaders to meet King Henry to name their grievances; they shall have their desires with interest and receive pardon absolute for having risen against him.

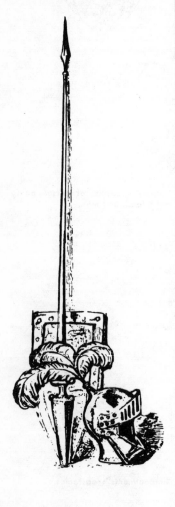

Hotspur thanks the king for this reasonable message, but goes on to recount how Henry owes what he has today to the help the Percies and others gave him when he landed with nothing on the shore at Ravensburgh. It is a long account, and Sir Walter Blunt did not come to hear speeches such as this.

Enter SIR WALTER BLUNT.

Blunt. I come with gracious offers from the king
If you vouchsafe me hearing and respect.
  Hotspur. Welcome, Sir Walter Blunt; and would to God
You were of our determination!   33
Some of us love you well; and even those some
Envy your great deservings and good name,
Because you are not of our quality,
But stand against us like an enemy.
  Blunt. And God defend but still I should stand so,
So long as out of limit and true rule
You stand against anointed majesty.   40
But to my charge. The king hath sent to know
The nature of your griefs, and whereupon
You conjure from the breast of civil peace
Such bold hostility, teaching his duteous land
Audacious cruelty. If that the king
Have any way your good deserts forgot,   46
Which he confesseth to be manifold,
He bids you name your griefs; and with all speed
You shall have your desires with interest
And pardon absolute for yourself and these
Herein misled by your suggestion.
  Hotspur. The king is kind; and well we know the king
Knows at what time to promise, when to pay.
My father and my uncle and myself   54
Did give him that same royalty he wears;   55
And when he was not six and twenty strong,
Sick in the world's regard, wretched and low,
A poor unminded outlaw sneaking home,
My father gave him welcome to the shore;
And when he heard him swear and vow to God
He came but to be Duke of Lancaster,
To sue his livery and beg his peace,
With tears of innocency and terms of zeal,
My father, in kind heart and pity moved,
Swore him assistance and perform'd it too.
Now when the lords and barons of the realm
Perceived Northumberland did lean to him,
The more and less came in with cap and knee;
Met him in boroughs, cities, villages,
Attended him on bridges, stood in lanes,
Laid gifts before him, proffer'd him their oaths,
Gave him their heirs as pages, follow'd him
Even at the heels in golden multitudes.
He presently, as greatness knows itself,
Steps me a little higher than his vow
Made to my father, while his blood was poor,
Upon the naked shore at Ravenspurgh;
And now, forsooth, takes on him to reform
Some certain edicts and some strait decrees   79
That lie too heavy on the commonwealth,
Cries out upon abuses, seems to weep
Over his country's wrongs; and by this face,
This seeming brow of justice, did he win
The hearts of all that he did angle for;   84
Proceeded further; cut me off the heads
Of all the favourites that the absent king

33. "determination": persuasion or beliefs.

40. "anointed majesty": reference to the sacred ritual of coronation and the divine right of duly anointed monarchs.

46. "forgot": forgotten (archaic past tense).

54. "father": Earl of Northumberland. "uncle": Earl of Worcester. "myself": Harry Percy (Hotspur).

55. "him": Henry Bolingbroke, then Duke of Lancaster.

79. "edicts": statutes, laws.

84. "angle": fish (for).

HENRY IV, 1

ACT IV SCENE III

Hotspur now reaches the point he is leading up to: Henry's refusal to ransom Mortimer. This is one of a long list of broken promises that they hold against the king, and they have also been investigating his claim to the throne and find his title too indirect for long continuance. They do not dismiss Blunt, but promise to send the Earl of Worcester to the king in the morning with their considered decision: meanwhile they will withdraw.

Hotspur even holds out the hope that they may agree to the king's conditions.

ACT IV SCENE IV

At the Archbishop's Palace in York, the Archbishop of York sends letters relating to the plot to the Earl Marshal (the Duke of Norfolk) and to his cousin Lord Scroop. These letters are very urgent, and Sir Michael says he guesses what they contain.

The Archbishop knows that the fate of ten thousand men will be decided at the battle which is to take place, he believes, at Shrewsbury tomorrow. He fears that owing to the absence of Northumberland and Glendower, Hotspur's army will prove too weak to overcome the majesty of England.

We hear that Mortimer is not there, but supporting the rebels are Mordake, Vernon, Hotspur, Worcester and a head of gallant warriors. The Archbishop is unconvinced; the King has gathered together a special army from the whole land, and is in a very strong position.

In deputation left behind him here,
When he was personal in the Irish war.   88
  Blunt. Tut, I came not to hear this.
  Hotspur.   Then to the point.
In short time after, he deposed the king;
Soon after that, deprived him of his life;
And in the neck of that, task'd the whole state
To make that worse, suffered his kinsman March,
Who is, if every owner were well placed,
Indeed his king, to be engaged in Wales,
There without ransom to lie forfeited;
Disgraced me in my happy victories,
Sought to entrap me by intelligence;
Rated mine uncle from the council-board;   99
In rage dismissed my father from the court;
Broke oath on oath, committed wrong on wrong,
And in conclusion drove us to seek out
This head of safety; and withal to pry
Into his title, the which we find   104
Too indirect for long continuance.
  Blunt. Shall I return this answer to the king?
  Hotspur. Not so, Sir Walter: we'll withdraw awhile.
Go to the king; and let there be impawn'd   108
Some surety for a safe return again,
And in the morning early shall my uncle
Bring him our purposes; and so farewell.
  Blunt. I would you would accept of grace and love.
  Hotspur. And may be so we shall.
  Blunt.   Pray God you do.   [*Exeunt.*

Scene four.

(YORK. THE ARCHBISHOP'S PALACE.)

Enter the ARCHBISHOP OF YORK *and* SIR MICHAEL.

  Archbishop. Hie, good Sir Michael; bear this sealed brief   1
With winged haste to the lord marshal;   2
This to my cousin Scroop, and all the rest
To whom they are directed. If you knew
How much they do import, you would make haste.
  Sir Michael. My good lord,
I guess their tenour.   7
  Archbishop.   Like enough you do
To-morrow, good Sir Michael, is a day
Wherein the fortune of ten thousand men
Must bide the touch; for, sir, at Shrewsbury,
As I am truly given to understand,
The king with mighty and quick-raised power
Meets with Lord Harry: and, I fear, Sir Michael,
What with the sickness of Northumberland,
Whose power was in the first proportion,
And what with Owen Glendower's absence thence,
Who with them was a rated sinew too   17
And comes not in, o'er-ruled by prophecies,
I fear the power of Percy is too weak
To wage an instant trial with the king.

---

88. "was personal in": attended in person.

99. "Rated": berated, drove out. "council-board": Council of State.

104. "title": claim to the throne based on line of descent etc.

108. "impawn'd" pledged.

1. "Hie": hasten.

2. "lord marshal": the earl marshal of England, the Duke of Norfolk.

7. "tenour": import.

17. "rated sinew": esteemed source of strength.

69

HENRY IV, 1

ACT IV SCENE IV

The Archbishop names the Prince of Wales and his brother, Prince John (he calls him Lord John, but this is a mistake) of Lancaster along with noble Westmoreland and warlike Blunt as merely some of the excellent soldiers the king has on his side.

Sir Michael feels they will be well opposed by the rebels, but the Archbishop is fearful still. He fears that the King will call in at York on the way back to London, if he wins the battle, and the wily Archbishop has to be prepared for what may take place then. He is rallying the support of his friends by furious correspondence.

Sir Michael. Why, my good lord, you need not fear; There is Douglas and Lord Mortimer.

Archbishop. No, Mortimer is not there.

Sir Michael. But there is Mordake, Vernon, Lord Harry Percy
And there is my Lord of Worcester and a head
Of gallant warriors, noble gentlemen.

Archbishop. And so there is: but yet the king hath drawn
The special head of all the land together:
The Prince of Wales, Lord John of Lancaster,
The noble Westmoreland and warlike Blunt;
And many moe corrivals and dear men   31
Of estimation and command in arms.

Sir Michael. Doubt not, my lord, they shall be well opposed.

Arch. I hope no less, yet needful 'tis to fear;
And, to prevent the worst, Sir Michael, speed:
For if Lord Percy thrive not, ere the king
Dismiss his power, he means to visit us,
For he hath heard of our confederacy,   38
And 'tis but wisdom to make strong against him:
Therefore make haste. I must go write again
To other friends; and so farewell, Sir Michael.
[*Exeunt.*

31. "moe corrivals": more fellows-at-arms.

38. "confederacy": alliance.

HENRY IV, 1

The king's camp near Shrewsbury is bustling with preparations for the battle. The king and the Prince of Wales are discussing the weather; it is morning. Both men are confident of victory.

A trumpet sounds the parley, and the rebel Worcester enters accompanied by Sir Richard Vernon. The King greets him sternly but justly and accuses him of fomenting civil war.

The king asks Worcester if he is willing to return to the obedient orb in which he used to live, and give up being an exhaled meteor, that makes people fear some dreadful thing is going to happen to them (civil war). Worcester denies responsibility for the war, and the King says if you are not responsible for it whence comes it then? Falstaff interjects a flippant remark but is instantly reproved by the Prince.

Worcester then recounts that they were originally among Henry's most vigorous supporters and that according to the oath that Henry swore at Doncaster he did not intend to seize the throne but only the dukedom of Lancaster to which he was entitled.

ACT FIVE, scene one.

(THE KING'S CAMP NEAR SHREWSBURY.)

Enter the KING, PRINCE OF WALES, LORD JOHN OF LANCASTER, EARL OF WESTMORELAND, SIR WALTER BLUNT, *and* FALSTAFF.

King. How bloodily the sun begins to peer	1
Above yon busky hill! the day looks pale	2
At his distemperature.	
Prince. The southern wind	
Doth play the trumpet to his purposes,	
And by his hollow whistling in the leaves	
Foretells a tempest and a blustering day.	
King. Then with the losers let it sympathise,	
For nothing can seem foul to those that win.	

                   [*The trumpet sounds.*

Enter WORCESTER *and* VERNON.

How now, my lord of Worcester! 'tis not well	
That you and I should meet upon such terms	10
As now we meet. You have deceived our trust	
And made us doff our easy robes of peace,	12
To crush our old limbs in ungentle steel:	13
This is not well, my lord, this is not well.	
What say you to it? Will you again unknit	15
This churlish knot of all-abhorred war?	
And move in that obedient orb again	
Where you did give a fair and natural light,	
And be no more an exhaled meteor,	
A prodigy of fear and a portent	
Of broached mischief to the unborn times?	
Worcester. Hear me, my liege:	
For mine own part, I could be well content	
To entertain the lag-end of my life	
With quiet hours; for I do protest,	
I have not sought the day of this dislike.	
King. You have not sought it! how comes it, then?	
Falstaff. Rebellion lay in his way, and he found it.	
Prince. Peace, chewet, peace!	29
Worcester. It pleased your majesty to turn your looks	
Of favour from myself and all our house;	
And yet I must remember you, my lord,	
We were the first and dearest of your friends.	
For you my staff of office did I break	
In Richard's time; and posted day and night	35
To meet you on the way, and kiss your hand,	
When yet you were in place and in account	
Nothing so strong and fortunate as I.	
It was myself, my brother and his son,	
That brought you home and boldly did outdare	
The dangers of the time. You swore to us,	
And you did swear that oath at Doncaster,	
That you did nothing purpose 'gainst the state;	
Nor claim no further than your new-fall'n right,	
The seat of Gaunt, dukedom of Lancaster;	
To this we swore our aid. But in short space	

1. "bloodily": the sun's color betokens the slaughter in battle that will soon take place (pathetic fallacy).

2. "busky": bushy.

10. "such terms": as representatives of opposing forces.

12. "doff": discard or take off.

13. "ungentle steel": uncomfortable armor.

15. "unknit": unravel or take to pieces.

29. "chewet": jackdaw or chatterer (chough).

35. "posted": rode posthaste.

HENRY IV, 1

ACT V SCENE I

Henry, according to Worcester, broke the Doncaster oath when he claimed the throne. Afterwards he behaved ungratefully to the very people who had helped him to power, like the cuckoo which pushes the rightful birds out of their own nests. For these things they cannot forgive him.

Henry says they have indeed been proclaiming their grievances up and down the land, and have incited the people to revolt.

The Prince supports his father against Worcester. He says in both your armies there is many a soul that shall pay full dearly for this encounter, when they meet in battle. He sends a message to Hotspur, Worcester's nephew, telling him that he is the bravest and most honorable of foes, and that though Hal has himself been a truant to honor, yet he will meet Hotspur in single combat and save the blood on either side. It was a common practice for armies to choose representatives to fight, the winning side being declared the conqueror. In this way general carnage was avoided.

Henry IV intervenes, and says he will not permit his son to fight on behalf of the entire side. He asks Worcester to take the offer of the King's grace back with him, and come again to tell him what they decide then.

Worcester and the accompanying knight, Vernon, return bearing the King's fair offer. The Prince doubts that it will be accepted by the rebels because the Douglas and Hotspur both are so confident they can win.

The King tells every leader to return to his men, and prepare; for on the rebels' answer they will take the necessary action. Their cause is just, and God is on their side.

It rain'd down fortune showering on your head;
And such a flood of greatness fell on you
What with our help, what with the absent king,
What with the injuries of a wanton time,
The seeming sufferances that you had borne,
And the contrarious winds that held the king
So long in his unlucky Irish wars
That all in England did repute him dead:
And from this swarm of fair advantages
You took occasion to be quickly woo'd
To gripe the general sway into your hand;
Forgot your oath to us at Doncaster;
And being fed by us you used us so
As that ungentle gull, the cuckoo's bird
Useth the sparrow; did oppress our nest;
Grew by our feeding to so great a bulk
That even our love durst not come near your sight
For fear of swallowing; but with nimble wing
We were enforced, for safety sake, to fly
Out of your sight and raise this present head
Whereby we stand opposed by such means
As you yourself have forged against yourself
By unkind usage, dangerous countenance,
And violation of all faith and troth
Sworn to us in your younger enterprise.
King. These things indeed you have articulate,   72
Proclaim'd at market-crosses, read in churches,
To face the garment of rebellion
With some fine colour that may please the eye
Of fickle changelings and poor discontents,
Which gape and rub the elbow at the news
Of hurlyburly innovation:
And never yet did insurrection want   79
Such water-colours to impaint his cause;
Nor moody beggars, starving for a time
Of pellmell havoc and confusion.
Prince. In both your armies there is many a soul
Shall pay full dearly for this encounter,
If once they join in trial. Tell your nephew,
The Prince of Wales doth join with all the world
In praise of Henry Percy: by my hopes,
This present enterprise set off his head,
I do not think a braver gentleman,
More active-valiant or more valiant-young,
More daring or more bold, is now alive
To grace this latter age with noble deeds.
For my part, I may speak it to my shame,
I have a truant been to chivalry;   94
And so I hear he doth account me too;
Yet this before my father's majesty—
I am content that he shall take the odds
Of his great name and estimation,
And will, to save the blood on either side,
Try fortune with him in a single fight.
King. And, Prince of Wales, so dare we venture thee,
Albeit considerations infinite
Do make against it. No, good Worcester, no,
We love our people well; even those we love
That are misled upon your cousin's part;
And, will they take the offer of our grace,

72. "articulate": made known publicly in clear terms.

79. "insurrection": rebellion.

94. "truant": absentee.

HENRY IV, 1

ACT V SCENE I

All but Hal and Falstaff go out, and Falstaff says if you see me down in battle, please stand over me to give me protection. Only a colossus could stand over you, says Hal. Falstaff is evidently nervous about the forthcoming action, and wishes the day were already over. The Prince tells him he owes God a death, and leaves him.

Falstaff, alone, makes a famous speech in which he analyzes the notion of honor. Why should he risk death when death has not called on him? What spurs him on? Honor. What is honor? Can it set legs and mend other wounds? No. What is honor then, —a word? What is in this word honor, air? Who has honor, the man that died last Wednesday? Does he know honor now? No. He concludes that honor is neither for the dead, who cannot feel it, nor for the living, since it frequently kills them. He will have nothing to do with it. Honor is a mere sign or coat of arms; and so ends his system of questions and answers (catechism). This speech which ridicules the notion of chivalry and honor is in the same tradition as Cervantes' attack on honor in the novel, Don Quixote. By reducing a metaphysical concept (honor) to a puff of air (a physical reality) Falstaff establishes himself among the original empiricists and logical positivists. This speech is extraordinarily interesting from a philosophical viewpoint.

ACT V SCENE II

At the rebel camp, Worcester is talking seriously to Richard Vernon about the King's offer. The offer is so liberal and kind that Worcester feels it should be kept from Hotspur, because Hotspur would almost certainly accept it. Vernon disagrees, but Worcester argues that if Hotspur finds out and agrees to the offer, the Worcester faction will be all undone, since it is highly unlikely that Henry will tolerate his enemies once they are in his power. For treason is but trusted as the fox, who may be tame but inherits the wild tricks of his ancestors. Worcester does not err in likening himself to the fox.

Both he and they and you, yea, every man
Shall be my friend again and I'll be his,
So tell your cousin, and bring me word
What he will do: but if he will not yield,
Rebuke and dread correction wait on us,
And they shall do their office. So, be gone;
We will not now be troubled with reply:
We offer fair; take it advisedly.
                    [*Exeunt* WORCESTER *and* VERNON.
Prince. It will not be accepted, on my life:
The Douglas and the Hotspur both together
Are confident against the world in arms.
King. Hence, therefore, every leader to his charge:
For, on their answer, will we set on them:
And God befriend us, as our cause is just!
[*Exeunt all but the* PRINCE OF WALES *and* FALSTAFF.
Falstaff. Hal, if thou see me down in the battle and
bestride me, so; 'tis a point of friendship.
Prince. Nothing but a colossus can do thee that 123
friendship. Say thy prayers, and farewell.
Falstaff. I would 'twere bed-time, Hal, and all well.
Prince. Why, thou owest God a death.   [*Exit.*
Falstaff. 'T is not due yet; I would be loath to pay
him before his day. What need I be so forward with
him that calls not on me? Well, 'tis no matter;
honour pricks me on. Yea, but how if honour prick
me off when I come on? how then? Can honour set to a
leg? no: or an arm? no: or take away the grief of a
wound? no. Honour hath no skill in surgery, then?
no. What is honour? a word. What is in that word honour? what is that honour? air. A trim reckoning!
Who hath it? he that died o' Wednesday. Doth he feel
it? no. Doth he hear it? no. 'Tis insensible, then. Yea,
to the dead. But will it not live with the living? no.
Why? detraction will not suffer it. Therefore I'll
none of it. Honour is a mere scutcheon; and so ends 140
my catechism.   [*Exeunt.* 141

Scene two.

(THE REBEL CAMP.)

Enter WORCESTER *and* VERNON.

Worcester. O, no, my nephew must not know, Sir
    Richard,
The liberal and kind offer of the king.
Vernon. 'Twere best he did.
Worcester.   Then are we all undone.
It is not possible, it cannot be,
The king should keep his word in loving us;
He will suspect us still and find a time
To punish this offence in other faults;
Suspicion all our lives shall be stuck full of eyes;
For treason is but trusted like the fox,
Who, ne'er so tame, so cherish'd, and lock'd up,
Will have a wild trick of his ancestors.
Look how we can, or sad or merrily,
Interpretation will misquote our looks,

123. "colossus": gigantic statue with legs astride (like that that bestrode the bay outside Rhodes).

140. "scutcheon": shield on coat of arms.

141. "catechism": series of formal questions and answers to be learned by heart.

HENRY IV, 1

ACT V SCENE II

It is likely that Hotspur's trespasses will be forgiven as faults of youth and hot blood, but Worcester's own offences are the deliberate treasons of age and cannot be so lightly disregarded, or pardoned.

Worcester acknowledges that he has led Hotspur and the others into this rebellion, so "we, as the spring of all, shall pay for all." Therefore he proposes not to tell Hotspur of the King's offer, and Vernon weakly concurs with this decision. This is the most traitorous and dishonorable act in the entire play, the betraying of Hotspur by his own uncle, and fellowconspirator. It is ironic that such an honorable gentleman as Hotspur should be so betrayed.

Hotspur enters, and asks what the news is; Worcester says the King will do battle soon. They send Douglas to tell the Earl of Westmoreland that they will fight to the end, and Douglas dashes out to throw this defiance in King Henry's teeth.

And we shall feed like oxen at a stall,
The better cherish'd still the nearer death.
My nephew's trespass may be well forgot;
It hath the excuse of youth and heat of blood,
And an adopted name of privilege,
A hare-brain'd Hotspur, govern'd by a spleen: 19
All his offences live upon my head
And on his father's; we did train him on,
And, his corruption being ta'en from us,
We, as the spring of all, shall pay for all.
Therefore, good cousin, let not Harry know
In any case, the offer of the king.
  Vernon. Deliver what you will; I'll say 'tis so.
Here comes your cousin.

       Enter HOTSPUR *and* DOUGLAS.

Hotspur. My uncle is return'd:
Deliver up my Lord of Westmoreland.
Uncle, what news?
  Worcester. The king will bid you battle presently.
  Douglas. Defy him by the Lord of Westmoreland.
  Hotspur. Lord Douglas, go you and tell him so.
  Douglas. Marry, and shall, and very willingly.
                          [*Exeunt.*
  Worcester. There is no seeming mercy in the king.
  Hotspur. Did you beg any? God forbid.
  Worcester. I told him gently of our grievances,
Of his oath-breaking; which he mended thus,
By now forswearing that he is forsworn:
He calls us rebels, traitors; and will scourge
With haughty arms this hateful name in us.

       Re-enter DOUGLAS.

Douglas. Arm, gentlemen; to arms! for I have
    thrown
A brave defiance in King Henry's teeth,
And Westmoreland, that was engaged, did bear it;
Which cannot choose but bring him quickly on.
  Worcester. The Prince of Wales stepp'd forth before the king,
And, nephew, challenged you to single fight.
  Hotspur. O, would the quarrel lay upon our heads,
And that no man might draw short breath to-day
But I and Harry Monmouth! Tell me, tell me,
How show'd his tasking? seem'd it in contempt?   51

Worcester tells Hotspur that the Prince of Wales stepped out before the King and challenged Hotspur to single combat. Hotspur is delighted and relishes the approaching fight with the King's own son. He asks whether the Prince asked for the fight in contempt, and Vernon says no, he never heard a challenge given more modestly, more like brother challenging brother. He gave Hotspur all the duties of a man, trimmed up his praises with a princely tongue, and chide his truant youth with so much grace, he made an excellent showing for himself.

  Vernon. No, by my soul; I never in my life
Did hear a challenge urged more modestly,
Unless a brother should a brother dare
To gentle exercise and proof of arms.
He gave you all the duties of a man:
Trimm'd up your praises with a princely tongue,
Spoke your deservings like a chronicle,
Making you ever better than his praise
By still dispraising praise valued with you;
And, which became him like a prince indeed,
He made a blushing cital of himself;
And chid his truant youth with such a grace
As if he master'd there a double spirit
Of teaching and of learning instantly.
There did he pause: but let me tell the world,
If he outlive the envy of this day,
England did never owe so sweet a hope,

19. "hare-brain'd Hotspur": note the derisive effect of the aspirate alliteration.

51. "contempt": The question reveals a touching desire in Hotspur to be well thought of by his foe, since they are brothers in honor despite their enmity.

HENRY IV, 1

ACT V SCENE II

Hotspur feels that Vernon is enamored of the Prince's follies, about which they have all heard a great deal, but longs for the time when they can match their skill and strength.

Calling them to arm with speed, Hotspur tells a messenger that he has no time to read the important letters that have just arrived. Another messenger enters, and says that the King comes on apace. Hotspur rejoices that the time of waiting is thereby diminished, and quoting the family motto (Esperance, Hope) and invoking the great name of Percy, he embraces his kinsmen and they go out to battle, to the sound of trumpets playing martial music.

ACT V SCENE III

On a plain between the two military camps near Shrewsbury the battle is already under way. In a golden suit of armor old Sir Walter Blunt impersonates the King. This was one of the ways the King himself was partly protected. The Scottish Douglas challenges him, says he has just killed Lord Stafford, and is about to slay King Harry. Blunt bravely takes him on, and is slain. Hotspur arrives and congratulates the Douglas on his manner of fighting. Douglas proudly claims he has killed the King, but Hotspur recognizes Sir Walter Blunt's features and tells Douglas of the mistake.

So much misconstrued in his wantonness.

Hotspur. Cousin, I think thou art enamoured   70
On his follies: never did I hear
Of any prince so wild a libertine.   72
But be he as he will, yet once ere night
I will embrace him with a soldier's arm,
That he shall shrink under my courtesy.
Arm, arm with speed: and, fellows, soldiers, friends,
Better consider what you have to do
Than I, that have not well the gift of tongue,
Can lift your blood up with persuasion.

Enter a Messenger.

Messenger. My lord, here are letters for you.

Hotspur. I cannot read them now.
O gentlemen, the time of life is short!
To spend that shortness basely were too long,
If life did ride upon a dial's point,
Still ending at the arrival of an hour.
An if we live, we live to tread on kings;
If die, brave death, when princes die with us!
Now, for our consciences, the arms are fair,
When the intent of bearing them is just.

Enter another Messenger.

Messenger. My lord, prepare; the king comes on
  apace.

Hotspur. I thank him, that he cuts me from my tale,
For I profess not talking; only this—
Let each man do his best: and here draw I
A sword, whose temper I intend to stain
With the best blood that I can meet withal
In the adventure of this perilous day.
Now, Esperance! Percy! and set on.   97
Sound all the lofty instruments of war,
And by that music let us all embrace;
For, heaven to earth, some of us never shall
A second time do such a courtesy.

[The trumpets sound. They embrace, and exeunt.

Scene three.

(PLAIN BETWEEN THE CAMPS.)

The KING *enters with his power. Alarum to the battle.*
Then enter DOUGLAS *and* SIR WALTER BLUNT.

Blunt. What is thy name, that in the battle thus
Thou crossest me? what honour dost thou seek
Upon my head?
Douglas.   Know then, my name is Douglas;
And I do haunt thee in the battle thus
Because some tell me that thou art a king.
Blunt. They tell thee true.
Douglas. The Lord of Stafford dear to-day hath
  bought
Thy likeness, for instead of thee, King Harry,
This sword hath ended him: so shall it thee,
Unless thou yield thee as my prisoner.
Blunt. I was not born a yielder, thou proud Scot;

---

70. "enamoured on": in love with.

72. "libertine": person without moral restraints.

97. "Esperance": Hope On, the family motto of the Percies.
"Percy": It was usual to invoke the great family name before taking action (a primitive form of ancestor-worship not confined to the Chinese).

HENRY IV, 1

ACT V SCENE III

Douglas is ashamed to have been made a fool of, and when he learns that King Henry has many men marching in his golden armor, threatens to slay the whole royal wardrobe.

As they go out to fight further, Falstaff comes in from the opposite side, saying that though he could avoid paying the reckoning in London, he fears the reckoning here, for in battle the only reckoning is paid in wounds. This is made with puns on shot (bill and bullet) and pate (plate, head).

Falstaff finds the dead body of Blunt, and says there's honor for you (this recalls the mischievous cynicism of his previous honor speech). He has led his own troops ("ragamuffins") where they were peppered with shot, so that only three were left alive, and these are so wounded that they will have to beg at the town's outskirts in order to live from now on. The Prince enters, and finds Falstaff standing idle there. He wants to borrow Falstaff's sword. Many noblemen's deaths are as yet unrevenged.

Falstaff claims he has done deeds this day that Turk Gregory himself never did, but he refuses to lend his sword and offers a pistol instead.

He is amazed to find the pistol still in its case. Falstaff warns him it is a special pistol, one fit to SACK a city, and as the Prince opens the case he finds inside not a pistol but a bottle of sack. He does not find the joke very funny at this time, and throws the bottle at Falstaff, who ducks and neatly catches it before it breaks.

Falstaff is left alone on the battlefield, and puns on the name of PERCY saying that he will PIERCE him. He hopes honor will not visit him in the same form that it visited Sir Walter Blunt.

And thou shalt find a king that will revenge
Lord Stafford's death.

    [They fight. DOUGLAS *kills* BLUNT.

    Enter HOTSPUR.

Hotspur. O Douglas, hadst thou fought at Holmedon thus,
I never had triumph'd upon a Scot.
Douglas. All's done, all's won; here breathless lies the king.
Hotspur. Where?
Douglas. Here.
Hotspur. This, Douglas? no: I know this face full well:
A gallant knight he was, his name was Blunt;
Semblably furnish'd like the king himself.   21
Douglas. A fool go with thy soul, whither it goes!
A borrow'd title hast thou bought too dear:
Why didst thou tell me that thou wert a king?
Hotspur. The king hath many marching in his coats.
Douglas. Now, by my sword, I will kill all his coats;   26
I'll murder all his wardrobe, piece by piece,   27
Until I meet the king.
Hotspur.   Up, and away!
Our soldiers stand full fairly for the day.   *[Exeunt.*
    Alarum. Enter FALSTAFF, *solus.*
Falstaff. Though I could 'scape shot-free at London,
I fear the shot here; here's no scoring but upon the pate. Soft? who are you? Sir Walter Blunt: there's honour for you! here's no vanity! I am as hot as molten lead, and as heavy too: God keep lead out of me! I need no more weight than mine own bowels. I have led my ragamuffins where they are peppered: there's not three of my hundred and fifty left alive; and they are for the town's end, to beg during life. But who comes here?

     Enter the PRINCE.

Prince. What, stand'st thou idle here? lend me thy sword:
Many a nobleman lies stark and stiff
Under the hoofs of vaunting enemies,
Whose deaths are yet unrevenged: I prithee, lend me thy sword.
Falstaff. O Hal, I prithee, give me leave to breathe awhile. Turk Gregory never did such deeds in arms   45
as I have done this day. I have paid Percy, I have made him sure.
Prince. He is, indeed; and living to kill thee. I prithee, lend me thy sword.
Falstaff. Nay, before God, Hal, if Percy be alive, thou get'st not my sword; but take my pistol, if thou wilt.
Prince. Give it me; what, is it in the case?
Falstaff. Ay, Hal; 'tis hot, 'tis hot; there's that will sack a city.   55
   [The Prince draws it out, and finds it to be a bottle of sack.
Prince. What, is it a time to jest and dally now?
   [He throws the bottle at him. Exeunt.
Falstaff. Well, if Percy be alive, I'll pierce him. If   57
he do come in my way, so: if he do not, if I come in

---

21. "Semblably furnish'd": dressed in armor to resemble the King.

26-27. "coats . . . wardrobe": sustained figure (becoming metaphorical).

45. "Turk Gregory": actually Pope Gregory VII, whose reputation for cruelty was like the Turks'.

55. "sack": loot and pilfer and, of course, the wine of this name also.

57. "Percy . . . pierce him": play on the name of the enemy; the name was probably pronounced Piercy in those days, which fact makes the pun more obvious.

76

HENRY IV, 1

ACT V SCENE IV

On another part of the field, King Harry entreats the Prince to leave the field because he is bleeding so badly. He tells Hal's brother John to go with him. Hal refuses to leave, and so does young Lancaster. The king tells Westmoreland to lead Hal to his tent, but Hal says he does not need any help. It is only a shallow scratch, he says, not enough to drive him from the field at a time when so many of his friends lie unrevenged.

Young Prince John leads his cousin Westmoreland back to the heart of the battle, and Hal praises his spirit to the King, who is indeed very proud of his two sons. The Douglas enters, spies Henry, and challenges him; the King admits his identity, and Douglas tackles him. He has been fooled once already, and is not going to make the same mistake twice. Yet this opponent bears himself like a king, and he is sure he will slay him. He almost does, for King Henry is old and quite feeble; the King is in danger of his life when the Prince of Wales reenters and takes on the Douglas, thereby releasing the King and undoubtedly saving his life.

his willingly, let him make a carbonado of me. I 59
like not such grinning honour as Sir Walter hath:
give me life: which if I can save, so; if not, honour
comes unlooked for, and there's an end. [*Exeunt.*

Scene four.

(ANOTHER PART OF THE FIELD.)

Alarum. Excursions. Enter the KING, *the* PRINCE, LORD
JOHN OF LANCASTER *and the* EARL OF WESTMORELAND.
King. I prithee,
Harry, withdraw thyself; thou bleed'st too much.
Lord John of Lancaster, go you with him.
Lancaster. Not I, my lord, unless I did bleed too.
Prince. I beseech your majesty, make up,
Lest your retirement do amaze your friends.
King. I will do so,
My Lord of Westmoreland, lead him to his tent.
Westmoreland. Come, my lord, I'll lead you to your
tent.
Prince. Lead me, my lord? I do not need your
help:
And God forbid a shallow scratch should drive
The Prince of Wales from such a field as this,
Where stain'd nobility lies trodden on,
And rebels' arms triumph in massacres!
Lancaster. We breathe too long; come, cousin West-
moreland,
Our duty this way lies; for God's sake, come.
[*Exeunt* LORD JOHN *and* WESTMORELAND.
Prince. By God, thou hast deceived me, Lancaster; 17
I did not think thee lord of such a spirit:
Before, I loved thee as a brother, John;
But now, I do respect thee as my soul.
King. I saw him hold Lord Percy at the point
With lustier maintenance than I did look for
In such an ungrown warrior.
Prince.   O, this boy
Lends mettle to us all!   [*Exeunt.*

Enter DOUGLAS.

Douglas. Another king! they grow like Hydra's 25
heads:
I am the Douglas, fatal to all those
That wear those colours on them: what are thou,
That counterfeit'st the person of a king?
King. The king himself; who, Douglas, grieves at
heart
So many of his shadows thou hast met
And not the very king. I have two boys
Seek Percy and thyself about the field:
But, seeing thou fall'st on me so luckily,
I will assay thee: so, defend thyself.
Douglas. I fear thou art another counterfeit; 35
And yet, in faith, thou bear'st thee like a king:

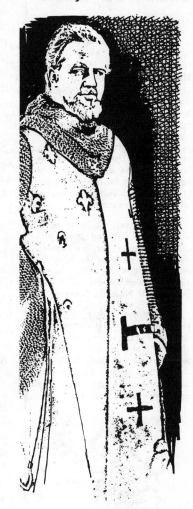

59. "carbonado": joint of meat slashed for broiling.

17. The deception referred to here is the concealing of a virtue; Hal is delighted at his brother's brave and manly performance during battle.

25. "Hydra's heads": Hercules slew this many-headed monster which grew two heads the moment one of them was cut off.

35. "counterfeit": fraud, masquerading as the King.

HENRY IV, 1

ACT V SCENE IV

The Prince knows that Douglas has already slain three of the king's men, Shirley, Stafford, and Blunt, and is determined to put an end to this. They fight, when the Douglas suddenly turns and flees for his life. Hal turns to his father, who is resting nearby, and asks him how he is. He has sent for aid and so has Clifton. The King says that Hal has redeemed the lost opinion he had of him, and has shown that he has a care for his father's life in the fair rescue he has just performed.

The Prince says his father never should have believed those who said he wished for his father's death; then he helps the King up, and Henry goes to Clifton to see about reinforcements, while Hal goes to Sir Nicholas Gawsey.

The moment when the two young men meet is now here; Hotspur and Hal meet, and it is clear, as Hal expresses it, that the two stars cannot keep their motion in one sphere. Similarly one of them has to go; which they now proceed to decide.

As they fight, Falstaff, who has just entered, cheers Hal on. Suddenly the Douglas enters and takes on Falstaff; two fights are going on simultaneously, one serious and proper, with two honorable men fighting for their lives, the other a parody of fighting, with Falstaff being chased and hit on the rump by Douglas's flat sword. Falstaff cannot run far, and soon falls down as if dead. As the Douglas makes off, Hotspur falls down, wounded. He says that Harry has robbed him of his youth. He, Percy, is now dust and food for . . .

Hal has to finish the sentence for him, since Hotspur is dead. He grieves for him as for a brother.

But mine I am sure thou art, whoe'er thou be,
And thus I win thee.

> [*They fight; the King being in*
> *danger, re-enter* PRINCE OF WALES.*

Prince. Hold up thy head, vile Scot, or thou art like
Never to hold it up again! the spirits
Of valiant Shirley, Stafford, Blunt, are in my arms:
It is the Prince of Wales that threatens thee;
Who never promiseth but he means to pay.

> [*They fight:* DOUGLAS *flies.*

Cheerly, my lord: how fares your grace?
Sir Nicholas Gawsey hath for succor sent,
And so hath Clifton: I'll to Clifton straight.
King. Stay, and breathe awhile:
Thou hast redeem'd thy lost opinion,   48
And show'd thou makest some tender of my life,
In this fair rescue thou has brought to me.
Prince. O God! they did me too much injury
That ever said I hearken'd for your death.
If it were so, I might have let alone
The insulting hand of Douglas over you,
Which would have been as speedy in your end
As all the poisonous potions in the world
And saved the treacherous labour of your son.
King. Make up to Clifton: I'll to Sir Nicholas
Gawsey.   [*Exeunt.*

Enter HOTSPUR

Hotspur. If I mistake not, thou art Harry Monmouth.
Prince. Thou speak'st as if I would deny my name.
Hotspur. My name is Harry Percy.
Prince.   Why, then I see
A very valiant rebel of the name.
I am the Prince of Wales; and think not, Percy
To share with me in glory any more:
Two stars keep not their motion in one sphere;
Nor can one England brook a double reign,   66
Of Harry Percy and the Prince of Wales.
Hotspur. Nor shall it, Harry; for the hour is come
To end the one of us; and would to God
Thy name in arms were now as great as mine!
Prince. I'll make it greater ere I part from thee,
And all the budding honours on thy crest
I'll crop, to make a garland for my head.
Hotspur. I can no longer brook thy vanities.

> [*They fight.*

Enter FALSTAFF

Falstaff. Well said, Hal! to it, Hal! Nay, you shall find no boy's play here, I can tell you.
Re-enter DOUGLAS; *he fights with* FALSTAFF, *who falls down as if he were dead, and exit* DOUGLAS. HOTSPUR *is wounded and falls.*
Hotspur. O, Harry, thou hast robb'd me of my youth!
I better brook the loss of brittle life
Than those proud titles thou hast won of me;
They wound my thoughts worse than thy sword my flesh;
But thought's the slave of life, and life time's fool;

48. "redeem'd thy lost opinion": proved himself a loyal son and a patriotic Englishman.

66. "brook a double reign": stand or put up with the two brilliant young men.

HENRY IV, 1

ACT V SCENE IV

He makes a brief funeral speech over Hotspur's body, in which he praises his courtesy but not his impulsiveness.

Then he spies the body (as he thinks it, dead) of Falstaff over there, and goes over saying he could have better spared a better man. He would have had a heavy miss of Falstaff if he had been much in love with vanity, but now (he implies) he will not miss him too much since he has reformed.

He promises to come back and embalm Falstaff later (the word used is embowell). As Hal leaves, Falstaff rises from the ground shaking somewhat at the dreadful thought of being embalmed. He says it was time to lie down, otherwise he would have been killed by the Douglas, that termagant Scot.

Falstaff eyes the body of Hotspur, and wonders whether he is really dead or counterfeiting. He grows distinctly nervous at the thought of Hotspur's rising from the earth again and, to prevent this, he takes his dagger and stabs the dead Hotspur in the thigh. Then, confident that Hotspur cannot move again, he takes the body up on his back, and is found carrying the corpse by Prince Hal and his brother John when they reenter a few moments later.

Hal congratulates John on the courageous way in which he has flesh'd his maiden sword (note the metaphor), using terminology that comes naturally to two healthy young men. Much Elizabethan language reveals a similar earthy concern with sensuality.

They are amazed to see Falstaff upright and apparently alive. Fal-

And time, that takes survey of all the world,
Must have a stop. O, I could prophesy,
But that the earthy and cold hand of death
Lies on my tongue: no Percy, thou art dust,
And food for—   [*Dies.*
    Prince. For worms, brave Percy: fare thee well,
        great heart!
Ill-weaved ambition, how much art thou shrunk!   88
When that this body did contain a spirit,
A kingdom for it was too small a bound;
But now two paces of the vilest earth
Is room enough: this earth that bears thee dead
Bears not alive so stout a gentleman.
If thou wert sensible of courtesy,   94
I should not make so dear a show of zeal:
But let my favours hide thy mangled face;
And, even in thy behalf, I'll thank myself
For doing these fair rites of tenderness.
Adieu, and take thy praise with thee to heaven!
Thy ignominy sleep with thee in the grave,   100
But not remember'd in thy epitaph!
                [*He spieth* FALSTAFF *on the ground.*
What, old acquaintance! could not all this flesh
Keep in a little life? Poor Jack, farewell!
I could have better spared a better man:
O' I should have a heavy miss of thee,
If I were much in love with vanity!
Death hath not struck so fat a deer to-day,
Though many dearer, in this bloody fray.
Embowell'd will I see thee by and by: 109
Till then in blood by noble Percy lie.   [*Exeunt.*
    Falstaff. [*Rising up*] Embowelled! if thou embowel
me to-day, I'll give you leave to powder me and eat
me to-morrow. 'Sblood, 't was time to counterfeit or
that hot termagant Scot had paid me scot and lot   114
too. Counterfeit? I lie, I am no counterfeit: to die is
to be a counterfeit for he is but the counterfeit of a
man who hath not the life of a man: but to counterfeit dying, when a man thereby liveth, is to be no
counterfeit, but the true and perfect image of life indeed. The better part of valour is discretion; in the
which better part I have saved my life. 'Zounds, I am
afraid of this gunpowder Percy, though he be dead:
how, if he should counterfeit too and rise? by my
faith, I am afraid he would prove the better counterfeit. Therefore I'll make him sure; yea, and I'll
swear I killed him. Why may not he rise as well as
I? Nothing confutes me but eyes, and nobody sees
me. Therefore, sirrah [*stabbing him*], with a new
wound in your thigh, come you along with me.
                [*Takes up* HOTSPUR *on his back.*
    Re-enter the PRINCE OF WALES, *and* LORD JOHN OF
                LANCASTER.
Prince. Come, brother John; full bravely hast thou
flesh'd thy maiden sword.
Lancaster.   But, soft! whom have we here?
Did you not tell me this fat man was dead?
    Prince. I did; I saw him dead,
Breathless and bleeding on the ground. Art thou
        alive?

88. "Ill-weaved ambition": a fitting epitaph; it was Worcester who contributed most to this ill-weaving of Hotspur's career.

94. "sensible of": aware of.

100. "ignominy": shame (of having been on the rebellious side).

109. "Embowell'd": embalmed.

114. "termagant": violent.

ACT V SCENE IV

staff throws down the body of Hotspur and claims to be made either earl or duke for having slain this foe.

Hal explains that he himself killed Percy, and left him lying dead on the ground next to Falstaff, but Falstaff says that after the Prince went out, Hotspur got up and they fought for one hour by Shrewsbury clock. Falstaff swears he gave Hotspur this wound in the thigh, and he certainly did (after Hotspur was dead, a fact not mentioned at this time).

Prince John declares this is the strangest tale he ever heard, and Hal says it involves the strangest fellow (Falstaff). To show that he is still kindly disposed towards Falstaff for the sake of old times, he says:

If a lie may do thee grace, I'll gild it with the happiest terms I have.

A trumpet sounds the retreat; the King's side has won the battle. Hal and his brother go off to the top of the field to see what the casualties are.

Falstaff follows them, for the reward. He vows to purge, and leave sack, and live cleanly as a nobleman should, if he is elevated to that state.

ACT V SCENE V

On another part of the battlefield, the King addresses his sons, the Earl of Westmoreland, and the prisoners, most notable of whom is the Earl of Worcester; Vernon is also among the prisoners. Thus ever, says the King, did rebellion find rebuke. He blames Worcester for most of the plot.

King Henry then gives the order to have Worcester and Vernon taken out and executed. Other offenders will be dealt with later.

The Earl of Douglas fled when he saw the tide turn against him, but fell from a hill and was so bruised that he was captured, and now sits in Hal's tent. He asks the King's permission to deal with him, and the King gladly grants

Or is it fantasy that plays upon our eyesight?
I prithee, speak; we will not trust our eyes
Without our ears: thou art not what thou seem'st.

Falstaff. No, that's certain; I am not a double man:
but if I be not Jack Falstaff, then am I a Jack. There
is Percy [*Throwing the body down*]: if your father
will do me any honour, so; if not, let him kill the
next Percy himself. I look to be either earl or duke,
I can assure you.

Prince. Why, Percy I killed myself and saw thee
dead.

Falstaff. Didst thou? Lord, Lord, how this world is
given to lying! I grant you I was down and out of
breath; and so was he: but we rose both at an instant and fought a long hour by Shrewsbury clock. If
I may be believed, so; if not, let them that should
reward valour bear the sin upon their own heads. I'll
take it upon my death, I gave him this wound in the 153
thigh: if the man were alive and would deny it,
'zounds, I would make him eat a piece of my sword.

Lancaster. This is the strangest tale that ever I
    heard.

Prince. This is the strangest fellow, brother John.
Come, bring your luggage nobly on your back:
For my part, if a lie may do thee grace,
I'll gild it with the happiest terms I have.   160
                    [*A retreat is sounded.*
The trumpet sounds retreat; the day is ours.
Come, brother, let us to the highest of the field,
To see what friends are living, who are dead.
        [*Exeunt* PRINCE OF WALES *and* LANCASTER.
Falstaff. I'll follow, as they say, for reward. He that
reward me, God reward him! If I do grow great, I'll
grow less; for I'll purge, and leave sack, and live
cleanly as a nobleman should do.   [*Exeunt.*

Scene five.

(ANOTHER PART OF THE FIELD.)

The trumpets sound. Enter the KING, PRINCE OF WALES,
LORD JOHN OF LANCASTER, EARL OF WESTMORELAND,
    with WORCESTER *and* VERNON *prisoners.*

King. Thus ever did rebellion find rebuke.
Ill-spirited Worcester! did we not send grace,
Pardon and terms of love to all of you?
And wouldst thou turn our offers contrary?
Misuse the tenour of thy kinsman's trust?
Three knights upon our party slain to-day,
A noble earl and many a creature else
Had been alive this hour,
If like a Christian thou hadst truly borne
Betwixt our armies true intelligence.   10
    Worcester. What I have done my safety urged
        me to;
And I embrace this fortune patiently,
Since not to be avoided it falls on me.

153. A lie can contain a limited amount of truth, and still be false.

160. "gild": endorse.

10. "true intelligence": accurate information.

HENRY IV, 1

ACT V SCENE V

this. Lancaster immediately goes off to release the Douglas without ransom, since they all admire him for the brave deeds he did before he realized the uselessness of fighting any **more.**

King Henry divides his army between Prince John and himself. Prince John and Westmoreland are to take their army to York, to deal with Northumberland and the Archbishop, Scroop.

King Henry, Prince Harry (Hal) and the rest are marching to Wales, there to attack Owen Glendower and the Earl of March. He vows to put down rebellion wherever it breaks out. He will not leave off the fighting until all his own has been won.

The mopping-up operation continues in Henry IV, Part II, and in the sequel, Henry V, Hal comes into his own.

King. Bear Worcester to the death and Vernon too:
Other offenders we will pause upon.

        [*Exeunt* VERNON *and* WORCESTER *guarded.*
How goes the field?

Prince. The noble Scot, Lord Douglas, when he saw
The fortune of the day quite turn'd from him,
The noble Percy slain, and all his men
Upon the foot of fear, fled with the rest;
And falling from a hill, he was so bruised
That the pursuers took him. At my tent
The Douglas is; and I beseech your grace
I may dispose of him.

King.   With all my heart.

Prince. Then, brother John of Lancaster, to you
This honourable bounty shall belong:
Go to the Douglas, and deliver him
Up to his pleasure, ransomless and free:
His valour shown upon our crests to-day
Hath taught us how to cherish such high deeds
Even in the bosom of our adversaries.

Lancaster. I thank your grace for this high courtesy,
Which I shall give away immediately.

King. Then this remains, that we divide our power.
You, son John, and my cousin Westmoreland
Towards York shall bend you with your dearest
    speed,
To meet Northumberland and the prelate Scroop,
Who, as we hear, are busily in arms:
Myself and you, son Harry, will towards Wales,
To fight with Glendower and the Earl of March.
Rebellion in this land shall lose his sway,
Meeting the check of such another day:
And since this business so fair is done,
Let us not leave till all our own be won.   [*Exeunt.*

NOTES

NOTES

CLIFF'S NOTES
COMPLETE STUDY EDITIONS

Shakespeare:

Hamlet	Merchant of Venice
Julius Caesar	Othello
King Lear	Romeo and Juliet
King Henry IV, Pt. 1	The Tempest
Macbeth	Twelfth Night

Chaucer's Canterbury Tales:

The Prologue	The Wife of Bath